(Welcome to) The Sh!t Club

A MALE'S PERSPECTIVE ON
STILLBIRTH, GRIEF AND LOSS

Jason Dykstra

"Jason's journey through grief is at the same time very personal but also re-latable to those who have experienced similar loss. His message of hope and reflection, as well as acceptance, should help others who find themselves in this (paraphrasing Jason) "awful club". I would recommend this book to those going through immeasurable loss, and to those who support these individuals as well."

Kathy Buckworth, Award-Winning Author of books like *I Am So The Boss of You* and Podcast Host of *Go To Grandma*

"This is an important book, sharing a journey of love, loss and healing that will help so many other parents who are members of this club that no one wants to be a part of. Jason's ability to relay his family's experience with com-passion and beautiful storytelling made it impossible for me to put this book down. I have no doubt that this book will open a conversation about loss and take away the stigma and hushed tones around this topic. It is a wonderful reminder that we are allowed to grieve, honour our losses, but it also gives us permission to still live a full and happy life."

Julie Cole, Co-Founder of Mabel's Labels and Best-Selling Author of *Like a Mother*

"This book will heal families! Jason's powerful, honest, and compelling story of losing his son reminds us that we have the capacity to hold both immense love and profound grief - the brutal with the beautiful. In a world where many men struggle to express and share their emotions, Jason's courage grants per-mission to befriend our own pain and sorrow, and to do so openly with others."

Sean Aiken, Co-Founder Rad-Dad Collective, Author of *One-Week Job Project*

"This book is so honestly and beautifully written. It shares what so many partners navigate through loss, often in silence. Jason's courage to share so vulnerably will, without a doubt, open up a much needed dialogue around the expectations we have of ourselves, our partners, and ultimately how families move through loss."

Aditi Loveridge, co-founder of the Pregnancy and Infant Loss Support Centre & Seeds of Growth

"Raw, rattling, and relatable. Any loss dad reading *(Welcome to) The Shit Club* will find themselves, throughout the pages, nodding in agreement or crying from visceral recollection. While every loss dad's story is unique, there are many relatable dynamics, emotions, and complexities that Jason articulates beautifully. Jason generously offers his readers a front row seat to his personal journey with loss and grief. Navigating grief doesn't come with a map; however, there is nothing more revealing than Jason's firsthand account of losing his son Ezra. Whether you're seeking validation as a fellow loss dad or the loved one of a loss dad hoping to grasp a greater understanding, there is something of immense value for you in this book."

Rob Reider, Co-Founder of the Sad Dads Club

"In a culture of men struggling to share their feelings, Jason steps outside of the pressure and courageously and generously invites us into his journey. By writing openly about his soul longings, fears, spirituality, and community, he cultivates more space to be human and share grief openly."

Dr. Karima Joy, Grief Researcher and Therapist

"*(Welcome To) The Shit Club* is a much needed partner's perspective of loss and grief in the pregnancy and loss community. Jason shares some hard truths of child loss and the impact of Ezra, at the same time, sharing about the community that supported his journey. Jason has an incredible ability to have the reader laughing and crying all at once. This book brought me back to the days and months after my daughter's death, reminding myself of the journey as we journey with Jason and his family."

Danyelle Kaluski, bereaved parent and co-founder of Pregnancy and Infant Loss Support Centre & Seeds of Growth

"A heartbreakingly beautiful memoir on love, vulnerability, community and grief. Jason reminds us that we are not alone as he recounts his experience of losing his stillborn son, Ezra, through the eyes of a father. This book is desperately needed in the Pregnancy & Infant Loss community and the world as a reminder that we are allowed to grieve in our own way and in our own timing. An absolute must read for anyone who has experienced a loss of this magnitude or is supporting others through this form of grief."

Melissa Sulley, Certified Pregnancy and Infant Loss Grief Coach and Founder of Josiah + Co.

"A must read! An empowering glimpse into a dad's soul through the most heartbreakingly beautiful journey of parenting both living and dead children."

Melissa Foley, Certified Pregnancy and Infant Loss Grief Coach and Founder of Lachlan's Light

Initial Edit: Hugh Cook
Production Editing: Kyle Kloostra
Text and cover design: Paper + Oats

Published by Seazens Collective
Life is brutal, life is beautiful; we're in this together.
www.seazenscollective.ca

Paperback Book ISBN: 978-1-7380091-0-7

Electronic Book ISBN: 978-1-7380091-1-4

For my earth-side and heaven-side kiddos.

Table of Contents

Introduction and Disclaimer

H ey there, and welcome. I'm sorry we've had to meet this way. You likely picked up this book because you are a card-carrying member of this genuinely shitty club. A club that I wish I could have the power to decline memberships, but a club that only seems to grow every single day. Or perhaps you picked up this book because you're supporting someone that joined this club (bless your heart). Regardless of why you're reading this, I'm sorry we had to meet this way, and yet, I'm still glad that our paths have crossed.

You should know a couple of things as you go into this book. I freaking hate journaling, and yet, I've been keeping some record of my life on a consistently inconsistent basis for many years. All that to say is that some of the details in this book are from those records, and others are the best recollection I have of these events. I believe them all to be accurate, but it's not out of the realm of possibility that I got a thing or two incorrect. Additionally, I have taken the liberty of changing some of the names of folks in the following pages either because I didn't think they would want to be named or I didn't want them to be identifiable.

Furthermore, the following pages depict one person's journey through a specific period of time. It's not the journey of my wife or any of our other family members; it's mine and mine alone. For full transparency, I wrote most of this book not even a year after our youngest daughter was born, meaning most of that year's memories were still fresh. While aspects of that person still exist, the person writing this now in 2023 differs from the person who originally penned some of these words. As such, some of my views (and theology) have changed. Some slightly and some more significantly. I wanted to be true to the person who wrote those words, so I have preserved them, as they were all heartfelt in those moments.

Lastly, this book does not prescribe what you should or should not be doing. Everyone's journey is unique, and this is a part of mine. I would encourage you to take what works for you and discard the rest.

A sincere thank you to the early readers of this manuscript: Amy, Melissa, and Keith; thank you for the time and energy it took to read and give valuable feedback on this book. Hugh Cook, for doing the initial edit all those years ago, and a massive thank you to my editor Kyle Kloostra for helping me mold this into something presentable. Thank you to Kelsey Baldwin from Paper + Oats for the beautiful design and attention to detail that is visually present throughout this book.

So much of this book is about community. I want to acknowledge some of the folks within my community that have significantly impacted my personal and professional growth by giving me the tools to assist myself and others through difficult times. Thank you, Glenn and Ros, from the Coping Centre, for giving me priceless advice and guidance many years ago that sent me down the path to where I am today. Aditi and Danyelle from PILSC, you have been incredible guides and supports in this journey, and I wouldn't be here without your continued support. A massive thank you to my grief coaching community, but especially to Melissa F., Melissa S., Annie, and Sue—you have shown me what it means to serve and love people in the roughest times of their life. To my colleagues, past and present, thank you, you know who you are.

Then there is our village; Benj and Amy, Russ and Melissa, and Jesse and Ang. You are an amazing group of people that have helped me (and us) in one of the most difficult seasons of our lives. While our journeys have all changed, I will forever be indebted to your kindness, love, and ability to show up in the darkness. Benj and Amy specifically, you need to be singled out for the amazing people you are—we would not be the people we are today if it were not for your continued friendship. You are our people.

A special thank you to our families for journeying with us over the years, providing guidance, and offering a supportive and listening ear (especially you, Denise!). My parents and in-laws, we could not have made it through without your love and support. We couldn't have done any of this without you.

We have leaned on our community since day one, and when we couldn't, you all showed up anyways—in the best of ways.

One of the main reasons I wanted to write this was to preserve these memories for my children, Carson, Zoey, Ezra, and Norah. While mostly Carson and Ezra are mentioned throughout the following pages, all four of you continue teaching me about life's beauties. Each of you, in your way, has expanded my heart more than you'll ever know. I'll die trying to show you the depths of this love. And finally, my incredible wife, Gina, who is my absolute rock and ride-or-die. We've been together through the most wretched and heartbreaking moments but also the most beautiful and joyous. It's amazing to me that now, more than 15 years in, I continue to love you more with each day.

CHAPTER 1

The Day I Became a Father

AUGUST 2010

T he day I became a father, I thought, everything will immediately change. I will leave my childish ways behind me and become this responsible adult—like what happened to Paul on the road to Damascus the day God showed up. I thought the miracle of birth might be my God moment. The baby will exit its growing station, get shoved into my arms, and instantly transform life. Now, I will start thinking of others more than myself, I will not have the urge to drink a few too many, and maybe I will finally quit smoking cigarettes. I will leave my life of vice and selfishness, becoming a real adult who cares for, loves, and nurtures this new little human creature.

But nothing changed. And everything changed.

Everyone told us that life would change when we first learned that we were expecting. Only no one told us that it wasn't an immediate change. When we informed our family that my wife had a little human growing in her, her brother's response was, "Your life is OVER!" He wasn't wrong, but he also wasn't right. My transformation didn't happen overnight, as with Paul. Mine was gradual—there was no shining light, there was no booming voice, there was no immediate difference. It's only in later reflection that you see these types of transformations.

When my wife, Gina, and I first got married we celebrated "thanks-for-not-making-me-a-father's-day." We would celebrate our freedom by buying something we didn't need, going out for supper, or watching a movie together. It was wonderful, having the freedom to do as we pleased when we pleased. And then I became a father.

That was seven years ago. I was working towards my dream of building my own business. Conflict management was my calling, and I was busy making connections and working on my mediation chops (not to be confused with meditation, of course). Those of you who start your own business know it doesn't just show up, so I was also working in a job I had started only 8-months prior. I worked as a Program and Volunteer Manager for a homeless and at-risk youth centre. I ran all the volunteers, the drop-in, and the new homeless shelter I had helped set up...all in 32 hours a week. It was a dream resumé building job, one of those jobs that give you a breadth of experience with various responsibilities and the title of being a manager. The staff I worked with was great, and the clientele taught me all about life. There was only one problem. My boss.

A few months after starting my job, I walked into my boss's office and asked if she was building up documentation to fire me. She had this unique way of complimenting me in person, and then reprimanding me in an email afterward. I never once received an email from her praising something that I did or even something with neutral content; the only ones I received were the tasks that were incomplete (even if those tasks were complete and we had just talked about them). She scoffed at the idea that she would be building up documentation to do something so heinous and told me that she wasn't used to someone taking the initiative I had taken in the few months I had been working there. She said my job was safe and that we were on good terms.

Immediately after that conversation, I received an email with some more tasks that I had (apparently) not done, with the rest of the organization cc'd. So, I did what most unhappy employees do...I started passively looking for a new job. After all, I needed something to give me experience and a decent paycheque as I began to build my own company.

Two days before our firstborn was due to be born, I got called into my boss's office. I had this funny feeling in my stomach as I walked across the hall toward her office. Entering the room, I could see that it wouldn't just be a conversation for the two of us as the Board Chair was sitting in the corner. *Oh crap,* I thought, *This can't be good.*

"Sit down, Jason," my boss said. "I'm sure you remember Rick, our Board Chair. I invited him to join us for this conversation."

Then she proceeded to fire me. "Rick will escort you to your office to grab your belongings and exit the building. You will not talk to any of your fellow employees or staff. You will not make any contact with them outside of this place either."

My head started swirling, and my vision started to fog. It felt like a bad drug trip happening in slow motion. I made my way to my desk with Rick directly behind me. I collected my things as my boss's thug looked over my shoulder to ensure I didn't take some crappy stapler, walked through the board room, and made my way down the stairs, walking past the drop-in centre where the rest of the staff were. I could feel their eyes focussing on me and the whispers start. I walked out of the building, to the small parking lot, put my stuff in the backseat, and got in the driver's seat.

I locked eyes with Rick as I got into my car. His eyes were full of pain and regret. "Sorry it had to work out this way, Jason," he said. I didn't respond and gave a slight nod, closed my door, and started my car. Two minutes down the road, I stopped at my favourite coffee shop and turned off the car. The tears began to form.

What am I going to do? I thought. We're supposed to have a baby in two days! How am I going to support my new family? How will I put food on the table for them? Gas in the car? A roof over our heads?

Thankfully, our baby was a bit of a procrastinator like me. The baby saw that due date and cruised through it for another eleven days. I started hustling to replace my job, and within five days of being fired, I was starting to schedule interviews with other organizations.

"Hi, Steve, yes I would love to apply to your organization and work for you....mmhhmmm....yeah....we can definitely do an interview....one thing, though, if I don't show up, it's because we're having a child.....yes......yes, it's our first....no, we're overdue with our child, so we're hoping any day now... yes.....yes, if for any reason I need to cancel the interview I'll do my best to give you a shout before I'm supposed to be there."

Eleven days after our baby's due date, we sat in the hospital, Gina hooked up to an IV with oxytocin pumping through the lines. Doctors and nurses were coming in and out of the room. Being in that sterile place reminded me of all the time I had spent in hospitals supporting clients during my time in social services. Though this was a little different, I wasn't getting paid, and it was my wife who was hooked up to the machines. And then it happened. Our child was born. As I held my son tightly in my arms, nothing else mattered. The world could have been falling apart, but I wouldn't know it. I was there with the biggest smile on my face. The upcoming interview, the past firing, and the worries all faded away as I stared into my son's eyes, and he looked up into mine. I was a father—his father. I would be there to protect him, provide for him, and be a role model for him.

Little did I know that I wouldn't have been able to protect him six years later. Little did I know that there would have been nothing I could have done to shield him from the pain that he would experience, that our family would experience.

CHAPTER 2

Our Devastating Blessing

AUGUST 2016

Six years later, the day of our devastating blessing started just like every other day. I stumbled out of bed before the kids woke up, hooked myself up to my IV filled with coffee, and sat down to read. In the heat of August, my wife was already 8 days overdue with our third child. We were in that routine of midwife appointments and weekly ultrasound appointments.

Just the day before, my wife went for another ultrasound at the hospital. Again, being the over-achiever that she is, she scored a perfect 8 out of 8 on her test. In other words, the baby was doing fine, my wife was doing well (albeit pretty tired), our other two children were very excited, and life, in general, was looking pretty good.

This whole being-overdue-thing wasn't new for us. Both of our other children were overdue as well, and we had to induce them to gently provide some encouragement for them to enter this beautiful world. Apparently, my wife has a comfortable womb! For both of our other children, we had a tried and tested plan around their anticipated arrival. Gina and I would schedule the induction date, and then we would go out for a date the night before our lives would be changed once again. We'd grab some supper, I'd have a beer, and she'd have a virgin daiquiri. We'd have a wonderful evening together and then go to bed to try and get some sleep...before we'd become (even more) sleep deprived again. The next morning, we would wake up, shower, grab some breakfast, and go to the hospital, where Gina would get hooked up to an IV with Oxytocin dripping through the lines. And then we'd wait. And wait.

With the news of a comfortable baby, we started making arrangements for our traditional pre-induction date as all signs pointed to another gently encouraged exit from the womb. So, that Friday morning, August 12, I woke up, fed the kids, and left for day two of a leadership conference I attended for work. As I sat there taking notes on the first speaker, my phone started to vibrate in my pocket.

"So...uh...I think I'm having contractions," read the text from Gina. My mind started to race. We had never experienced a "normal" birth! What was going to happen? Should I leave right now? How quickly would it happen? How was life about to change? Our youngest was already two and a half, and we were just in the process of leaving the diaper-life behind us. We had been running man-to-man defence long enough that I wondered how we would shift to zone defence. What have we done? How would we handle three kids running in different directions with just the two of us? How were we supposed to get three kids ready to go out? How were we going to raise and nurture another one?

I tried to make my text as cool and calm as possible "Okay...let me know when you need me to come home." Really, there wasn't much I could do at home. The contractions weren't very close together, and what were we supposed to do? Both just sit there twiddling our thumbs, waiting for the contractions to increase in intensity and frequency? Aside from that, I had already paid good money to attend this conference and wanted to ensure that I got my value out of it. After all, I'm a Dutch Canadian, and we love to get our money's worth!

A few hours later, the awaited text came: "Come home....I need you." I packed my stuff, told my friend that I had to run home to help out with the kids, and took off towards home. I swooped into the house like a superhero, finished feeding the kids their lunch, packed them up, and swept them off to my in-laws.

My mother-in-law took me aside when I arrived and asked, "You think this is a false alarm, Jason, or is it the real thing?" I shrugged my shoulders in response. "I have no idea," I said. After all, how was I to know whether this was a false alarm? This was the first time we had ever had a baby this way.

I sped out of the driveway back towards home, where Gina greeted me with some unwelcomed news. "The midwives just called, and they said the hospital is full. They're turning away people to surrounding hospitals. So, we have a few choices: we can go to one of those hospitals and get discharged from midwife care, or...we can have a home birth."

A home birth? I thought. *We're not prepared for something like that!* I had always told my wife that under no circumstances were we going to have a home birth, and she had agreed. We used to joke together that "you can wash the sheets, but you can't erase those memories."

However, she seemed quite confident that she wanted the midwives involved in this birth, so I said to her, "If you want to do a home birth, then we'll do that. It's up to you—either way, I support you." I was terrified of doing a home birth. What if something went wrong? What if we needed a doctor there? What if we didn't have all the right stuff that was needed?

"All we need is a couple of garbage bags," Gina said. *Ah, crap!* I thought. *We only have one left.* "I'm off to the store; anything else you need?"

Walking through the grocery store, I felt my stomach start to knot. *Three kids...three kids!* I began to think about all the things we could do as a family. I started to think about when our oldest son, Carson, would be in grade 5 and this new child would just be starting school. I thought about who was going to sit where in the van. Finally, I snapped out of my thoughts for a moment to pay the cashier before heading home.

The first midwife showed up at our house, laid my wife on the couch, and hooked up the ultrasound machine. *Whoosh, whoosh, whoosh,* whirred the machine as it frantically looked for a heartbeat. The machine wand tried to expel some magic as it searched Gina's stomach from top to bottom, from side to side. I briefly met my wife's eyes and gave her my best *It's-going-to-be-fine-babe* look. The wand scoured my wife's stomach, searching every square inch for that little noise—*b-bub, b-bub, b-bub, b-bub, b-bub.*

But it couldn't find one.

"Don't worry," the midwife said, "sometimes these machines can be a little finicky. We have another machine on the way."

Be strong, Jason, I thought. *She needs you right now. Ignore that feeling in your stomach. It's all going to be okay. It's all going to be okay. It's all going to be okay. Drive that feeling out of your mind, out of your stomach, out of your sight. There's another machine coming.*

Moments later, the second midwife walked into the house with another, stronger ultrasound machine. *Whoosh, whoosh, whoosh,* whirred the machine, again frantically searching for a heartbeat. My wife's eyes and mine met again as tears started to form. My stomach began to form knots. *Be strong, Jason; you're going to be needed.*

"911? Yes, we need an ambulance...yes....yes...13 minutes? Okay, thanks," the midwife said and hung up the phone. "I just got off the phone with the hospital, and they just had a room open up, so I called the ambulance to come bring us there. They'll be here in about 13 minutes."

"13 minutes? 13 minutes?" I said. "I can get to the hospital in 15; let's pack up and go."

"You okay to drive, Jason?" asked the midwives.

"Let's go," I said and grabbed the overnight bag we had packed for the hospital, and off we went.

Gina and I barely spoke in the car for the entirety of the trip. We just sat there, holding hands with my right hand, the other clutching the wheel and showing the white on my knuckles. The car slammed into park at the hospital 15 minutes later, and I hit the ground running before the vehicle had really stopped to grab a wheelchair for Gina. We wheeled up to the fourth floor, got in the hospital bed, and barely 10 minutes later, our baby was delivered.

Straight into the hands of God.

There was no sound, the machines blurred out, the people faded into the background, and there was the sickening sound of silence where there should have been a baby's first cry while he gasped for air.

Silence.

My mind went blank, my legs went weak, and I struggled to sit in the old tattered leather chair where the fathers before me had comfortably sat. Nobody said anything. There was the hustle and bustle around the room while my wife and I just sat there.

We didn't know if we were having a boy or a girl, and for the first time, we didn't have a really good guess either. For our other two children, I was sure that the first was a boy and the second was a girl. Everyone doubted me, especially on the second one. "Naa!" they said, "Look at the way she's carrying! Look at the heartbeat of that child! It's definitely going to be a boy!"

But I was convinced. Call it a father's intuition. Call it wishful thinking. Call it whatever you want, but I knew our second would be a girl. After our little girl was delivered, I did the routine calls to everyone, and my mother-in-law (God bless her) couldn't believe she was wrong about this. She was so convinced!

That's part of the fun of not knowing, though, isn't it? We like to guess and imagine what our children will be and how they will grow into their own. We love to imagine the difference in personality that they might have if they were a girl or a boy. We love to imagine the groups of friends they might have and to think about the differences we would experience when their friends came over. We love to guess and imagine the future.

If I'm being really honest with you, I flip-flopped a lot during this third pregnancy. One moment I had an overwhelming thought that the child would be a boy, and the next day I would think it was going to be a girl. I finally settled on a slight lean towards girl. And now, to my surprise, there lay my little boy...peacefully sleeping in God's arms. He looked so perfect. *No,* I thought, *he **is** perfect.*

I walked over to him as he lay on the weigh scale, the nurses and midwives doing their thing. I studied him through the tears streaming down my face as I looked at his little hands and his face. A voice shattered the silence, "What's his name?"

"Ezra William," we replied in unison.

As I sat in disbelief in the tattered leather chair, the nurse swaddled Ezra into a blanket and brought him over to me so I could hold him for the first time. She placed him in my, arms and I stared at his face. I began sweating profusely; I started shaking, and I wanted to throw him quickly out of my arms. I needed to get him out of my arms; I had to pass him on to someone else. But I couldn't. I couldn't stand, I couldn't talk, I couldn't bring myself to part with my baby boy. I slumped into the chair, a feeling of betrayal coming over me for even thinking those thoughts. I felt I had done something wrong to deserve this. I looked over to my wife, crumpled in the bed across the room as she lay there sobbing.

I let my hands run over his body; I traced his face with my fingers, fiercely trying to memorize every crease and crevice. Finally, I held his hand, praying for him to suddenly grab hold of my fingers.

Have you ever had to call someone when they expect good news from you?

"Hello? Jason! Do you have something to tell me?"

So much excitement, hope, and exhilaration steeped deep into their voice. I could hear them trying to claw through the phone so they could immediately transport themselves into my arms and hug me like an air mattress that's been pumped up to the point of explosion.

"I...uh...well..uh...hey there...our baby...he...he...he died...he was born without a breath...he was...a stillborn."

Every time those words were spoken, it was as if someone had slashed that overfull air mattress with the sharpest knife around, and you could hear and feel the rushing air pour out as the mattress crumpled to the ground. Then, gasps, cries, and more silence filled the air.

Making those phone calls, I became a little boy again. I just wanted my mom there. My parents had moved about three hours north of us a few years before, and this was the first time that I really felt the distance. "Oh Jay," she said, "I'm so sorry...your dad is at work right now...the dog...we need to get someone to take care of the dog...oh Jay...let me call your dad, and we'll start making our way down right now." I just wanted her with me immediately. I wanted to transport her right into that hospital room so she could hug me, tell me she was there for me, and that everything would be alright. Just like only a mother can.

Family and friends began to parachute into the hospital. Our friend Dina was one of the first people we called. Not only is she our friend, but she's also one of the pastors at our church. Dina was the first to show up, and after giving us hugs and embraces, she put on her pastor's hat and got down to work. She organized the people who walked into our room, so we didn't get overwhelmed. She started planning the funeral and arranged everything from funeral homes to who was going to officiate the funeral. She took care of everything we could possibly need for the next few days. She prayed with us, the midwives, and the hospital staff. She seemingly was able to do everything for everyone at that moment, and we would have been lost without her.

It became a rhythm; two or three people would walk into our little delivery room so they can meet our little Ezra. They held him, touched him, kissed him, took in his beauty, his perfection. Some said words of encouragement, some cursed, and some just sat there and cried as they gazed into his little eyes. Soon they got up, tears forever imprinted into their hearts, hugged us, and left the room to tell the next people it was their turn.

Then in walks Benji, his wife Amy, and our friend Ang. Benji walks straight up to me like he's on a mission and takes me into his arms. He grips me tight and draws me close, and I can feel the tears on his face. "Shit, man...I don't know what to say other than I'm so sorry, " he says. He holds on to me, and I can't bring myself to let go. Finally, we both sit down, and they pass Ezra delicately from one person to the next. "He's perfect," they say, "he's beautiful...wow, he looks so much like his brother and sister."

Then it's just us: my wife, our baby Ezra, and me. So, we sit on the bed for hours, holding, touching, and kissing his little face.

Dina walks into the room, and she looks exhausted. She's been working hard for us the last few hours, calling our transitional pastor, who had just left for vacation the day before, calls to the funeral home, and talking with all our family and friends. I give her a hug, "Thank you, D, for all your help today...we couldn't have done this without you." She gave us some things we'll need to think about for tomorrow, and I asked her if she can pray with us.

Dina joins the three of us on the bed and starts to pray. "God...oh God.... this sucks...this really sucks..." We sit there praying for a while, taking turns speaking words, crying out to God, sobbing, comforting each other, and being comforted.

I try to stay strong through everything. Through the prayer. But I can't be the hero this time. I can't fix this situation. I can't make things better. I can't repair anything. I'm helpless, totally not in control, and at the complete mercy of others and God. I just sit there comforting and being comforted. It's all out of our control.

We asked the nurses what had happened. We asked the midwives what had happened. We asked the doctors what had happened. But there's no answer. "We don't know for sure," they say, "and there's a good chance that we'll never know...there are a few guesses or theories, but...we're not sure." And so, we sit there holding our baby boy. We rock him back and forth as if he is being fussy, and we hold his little hand, taking his fingers into ours. We kiss him softly on the forehead and touch noses with him because that's a love you can never describe. We sit there on the delivery bed for hours, just gazing at him.

But we can't sit here forever. "Take as much time as you need," the midwives and nurses say. I never want to leave, but I don't think they'll accept me moving into the hospital room. We know we can't take him home with us, and that's the most painful thing. We sit there talking. "I don't want him to get tucked into the morgue by just anybody," Gina says. We plan to have the midwives bring Ezra down to the morgue because it doesn't feel right to have strangers tuck our baby boy in on his first bedtime. It doesn't feel right letting him out of our sight to sit in a hospital basement all by himself. It doesn't feel right that we should have to tuck our little boy into a bassinet and go home without him.

I look at the clock and see it's three in the morning. I speak the words that both of us are thinking, but neither is willing to say. "It's time to go." We don't have a lot of answers. We have no idea what happened to our precious child that day, and we'll likely never know. So we tuck him in the rolling bassinet, and we sing with him for the first and the last time his bedtime prayers:

Now I lay me down to sleep
I pray the Lord my soul to keep
Guide me through the starry night
And wake me when the sun shines bright.

Now I lay me down to sleep
I pray the Lord my soul to keep
If I die before I wake
I pray the Lord my soul to take.

Amen.

I stuff the rest of Ezra's things into the overnight bag, zip it shut, and grab Gina's hand as we walk blindly toward our van. As I open the side of the van to put the overnight bag in, there sits the base of the car seat. It was ready for him. Ready for us to take him home...but he wouldn't be joining us on this new chapter. I place the bag on top of the car seat base and close the door. It was time to go home.

It was a quiet ride home. There wasn't much to say other than the tears that streaked our faces and the occasional gasping for air. It was 4:00 a.m. by the time we got home. I opened the van door, grabbed the overnight bag, and brought it into the house. I stared at this bag that contained Gina's clothes and Ezra's soon-to-be belongings and slid it into our room. I walked into the kitchen and poured some drinks for us, wine for my wife, and a strong glass of whiskey for myself as we settled onto the couch. We were surrounded by silence. It pierced the air. There was nothing to say, nothing to do at that moment. So, we just sat there in disbelief. It all felt like a nightmare that we would hopefully wake up from soon.

The night offered us a few minutes of "sleep" until it was time to start a new day. It's amazing how your body goes into auto-pilot in these moments. Before we were fully awake, coffee was in the process of being brewed, we made breakfast, and I sat at the kitchen table surrounded by kids' colouring books and markers, wondering who had made these things for me. I wasn't hungry, and my eyes felt as if I had been repeatedly punched the night before.

I checked my phone and saw that I had gotten a text from Dina. "Hey, check in with Dean from the funeral home when you get a chance; they have a couple of questions about the funeral, but other than that, everything is just about ready for you." So, while Gina hopped in the shower, I gave him a call.

"Hello? Dean? Hi...it's Jason...ummm...I was told to contact you to talk about making arrangements for....arrangements for...ummm...it's Jason..."

"Hi there, Jason; thanks for giving me a call," Dean said. "First, let me express my deepest sympathies to you and your wife. Second, I just had a couple of questions for you...for starters, where are you planning on burying Ezra?"

Holy crap, I thought, *we have to bury our son.* I tried to explain some of our wishes, and Dean told me about the business of death. I told him about some of our hopes for timelines regarding the burial. He told me even more about the business of death and some of the politics around it. For example, did you know all the paperwork that you need to bury someone? Do you know how difficult it is to get any paperwork through on a Saturday? I held it together, now was not the time to break down. Now was the time to take care of business. Now was not the time to mourn; now was the time to be strong and to arrange the details. So, I put on my business hat and did what I had trained for many years to do. Negotiate. For nearly a decade, my job has been to help people develop as leaders and to manage or transform conflict situations. This was not the time for feelings; it was time for business.

"Thanks, Dean, I know that trying to arrange a funeral for tomorrow will be difficult, and I also know that you've been in this business for a while, and you come highly recommended. Thank you so much for the information that you have shared so far. You deal with the city a lot, I'm sure. Here's the thing, Dean, our pastor, will be here tomorrow, Sunday afternoon, and then he's gone again. That's the timeline we're working with here. So, we need to get in touch with the city to arrange these plots as soon as possible, and I'm sure because of your length of experience and expertise in this area you have some contacts there that you could get a hold of, even on a Saturday. So please help us get this done properly...and tomorrow."

Dean didn't protest; he just listened. There was a pause on the line. "Okay, Jason," he said after a moment. "I have a few favours that I can call in; let me see what I can do, but I can't make any promises. We'll see you here at the funeral home in a few hours."

I got down on my knees and prayed. "God...this really sucks. I'm not sure what's really going on here, but I'm going to need some help from you...It has to happen tomorrow. Please, God. Make it tomorrow, also...while we're on the subject, this fucking sucks, God. He's just a baby. He had so much to experience yet. So much life to live. So much...so much...Tomorrow, God...we need to get through today so we can get through tomorrow...what do you say, God?"

Thirty minutes later, my phone started to ring. "Hello? Jason? Hi, it's Laura from the city. Dean called us, and I'm so sorry for the loss. He said that you're looking to make sure the funeral happens tomorrow. Okay, so to do this, we'll need to decide where the plots will be. Would you have a few moments to come into our office and chat after you've been to the funeral home? Great, see you then." I hung up the phone, looked up, shut my eyes, and said, "Thank you, God."

Throughout each telephone conversation, I wrote notes furiously to ensure I didn't miss any detail or name. I poured some coffee for Gina, and we sat in our empty house to discuss each cemetery's advantages and disadvantages. "Well, this one looks like it backs onto the highway; that doesn't sound very peaceful....what about this one? It's decently close by, and look, some trains would go through the back of the cemetery..." As we talked, I studied Gina's face. Her eyes were bloodshot and puffed up from hours of crying, and she looked exhausted, and beautiful.

In 2017, Gina and I will celebrate our 10th wedding anniversary. Ten years! That's one whole decade! Though our story didn't start there. We met almost twenty years earlier at a baseball tournament in elementary school. She was interested in one of my best friends, Mark, at the time. We were just becoming aware that girls were interesting, so we bugged Mark a lot about Gina over that year. Just over a year later, I found myself sitting in Mr. Kamphuis' grade 9 geography class right next to Gina. Before I knew it, we were doing a project together and quickly became inseparable. We'd chat on the phone for hours when we weren't together, have sleepovers, and go to all the high school parties together. We never dated, and to be honest, I was terrified to date her.

I remember sitting on my parents' front porch a while, later talking to a friend who suggested I ask Gina out. "She's perfect for you! You guys know each other well; she's beautiful, and you obviously like her, so go out with her!" That's when I realized eventually; we'd get married. There was a slight problem, though. She was dating someone else. And over the next couple of years, when she wasn't dating someone else, I was. We couldn't really get our timing down. Even though we dated others, looking back on those years, it was pretty clear that my heart belonged to her.

I still remember our first kiss. I had recently returned from a couple of months of tree planting in northwestern Ontario, and Gina and I were hanging out for the day and then slept over at her parents' house. Just before bed, as we were talking in her room, she leaned towards me slightly, and we kissed. Then she left. I sat there in the dark thinking, *holy crap...I can't believe that just happened!*

There was some pressure on us from the beginning, as many people expected us to get married before we had even started dating. Comments like, "Just open your eyes, guys! You're made for each other!" But Gina and I never listened too much to others. We wanted to make sure it was right for us. So, for a while, we hid the fact that we were dating and didn't really tell anyone.

A few months later, on the first day of university, we celebrated my mom's birthday at my parents' house. We were standing outside having a beer with a mutual friend when he turned and said, "You know guys, everyone knows about you...why don't you just make it official already?" I looked at Gina, she looked at me, and we both smiled. The rest is history, as they say. We dated for three years before I asked her to marry me, which started a year-long engagement.

That morning we sat at our kitchen table, almost 15 years after we started dating, planning something that we had never expected to plan. A funeral. A funeral for our son. My eyes felt like a balloon that had been blown up and then ignored for a week. We sorted through Ezra's clothes that sat untouched in the dresser for something that would be fitting for a newborn to be buried in and the perfect blanket for him to be swaddled in.

We dabbed our eyes, started the van, and made our way to the funeral home to plan our son's burial. There we met both of our fathers. We knew the conversation would be tough and that we would need some physical and emotional support. We walked into the funeral home together, the place where people are readied to be lowered into the ground—the place where legacies are born. We talked through the details, signed the paperwork, and discussed how we wanted the funeral service to go. Dean and his colleagues at the funeral home held the perfect balance between compassion, empathy, and drawing out our wishes and expectations for the day. "Don't worry about a thing; we will coordinate with the pastor and work out all the details with him and Dina. We'll take care of it all." Leaving there, I was relieved to know that someone was going to take care of the details, the planning, and the coordination of the funeral so we didn't have to try and hold it all and make everything a bigger disaster.

Outside the funeral home, I hugged my dad. "I'm so sorry, son," he said through tears. "I'm...I'm not really good at these things. I can't stop crying, and that's probably not what you need right now."

I looked at him. "You being here is exactly what I need." I needed a surrogate tear-maker. I needed his physical presence of support. Having my dad and my father-in-law there that day, sitting in the funeral home, tears flowing from their eyes and staining their cheeks, they were crying for me so I didn't have to. I couldn't. I needed to be present and speak about the funeral details. I needed to concentrate on getting through the difficult details, making decisions on behalf of Gina and me, and concentrate on burying my son in a way that would honour him. I needed to be in control of my thoughts and emotions for those split seconds and moments, and having someone there who could cry on my behalf to give my eyes a much-needed break was precisely what I needed.

This was also a different side of my dad that I had not seen very often. It was the emotional support I had always craved. As I was growing up, my dad spent a lot of time at work, providing for his family. I have a lot of great memories of spending vacations with my dad and family, but not many with him from Monday to Friday. He was doing what men did at the time: putting food on the table. When he wasn't at work, he was getting ready for work or off to meetings for the various church and school committees he was on. It really wasn't his fault; he was doing what he needed to.

The four of us jumped into my father-in-law's truck and began making our way to the cemetery. It was raining as we rolled into the driveway. The water dribbled out of the sky, spreading its tears on the acres of green grass and tombstones that marked lives lived. Since it was Saturday, the office building doors were locked, so we walked around the property a little, looking at the markers other families had laid for loved ones and listening to the sounds of the rain sprinkling through the trees. The raindrops settled on our faces, joining the tears and washing away their sting. I called the lady we were supposed to meet, and she said to come knock on the office door. We followed her into the building and then into a little office.

"I'm so sorry for your loss," she began, "You're far too young to be experiencing this." We stared back at her dumbfounded. *Too young to experience this? Too young? What about our son? The one that didn't get to live to see his first birthday, his first week, his first day of life? What about our son, who didn't even get the chance to open his eyes and see his parents, that love him so much? What the heck do you know, lady, about what we've been through in this moment or any other?* I stuffed the responses down that I wanted to scream out at her and told her that we wanted three plots, one for Ezra's mom, one for his dad, and one for him. She drew up the paperwork and explained how it could be paid. "We want him buried right between us," we said. She fumbled around with the maps and apologized that it was a new lot that they were just finalizing the drawing for. She made several phone calls to ensure she had done the work correctly as we repeatedly said, "Please, just make sure that he gets buried in the centre plot, right between us."

"Yes, of course," she said, fumbling around with paperwork.

"Please, if you could just make yourself a note somewhere so that you remember amongst all the other details you're carrying," I said.

"Yes, that's a good idea," she replied.

We walked out to the plots we had chosen to make sure it was the right spot for our little boy and us. As we looked for the right markers that were hidden behind the grass, I looked around. Luscious, beautiful grass surrounded us. They had just opened up this plot of land, so there were virtually no graves or markers in this section. The spots we were looking at were right beside one of the roads that wound through the cemetery. The field across the road from us was full of tombstones, many marked with flowers, others with balloons, and others with various trinkets for the dead to take to their next life. I heard a train in the distance blowing its horn and thought, *yes...this is a good spot for our boy. He'd like it here.*

We got back in the truck and did the most difficult and wonderful thing that day: we went to see our other two children. They were still at my in-laws' place with all three of my sisters and their husbands, Gina's sister and brother, and their spouses. It was going to be a full house and completely overwhelming. The kids were so excited to meet the little baby that was growing in mommy's tummy, and now they wouldn't get that chance.

The kids and I, in the months previous, would imagine what the new baby was going to be like. Would it be a boy or a girl? What would the baby be like? What would it be like to have another brother or sister? When our oldest boy, Carson, would be in grade 4, how old would the new baby be? What about when Zoey was in grade 2? We would practice math and stretch our imaginations to what we would do with their little brother or sister. And now we had to explain to them that their brother, the one they greatly anticipated wouldn't be physically joining them in their life's journey.

As a parent, you want to be strong for your children. You want to be the one to comfort them, care for them, protect them from harm, and engulf them in love. As we approached my in-laws' driveway, I was shattered. The thought of seeing my two other children filled me with love so strong that it physically hurt. I felt as though I'd dropped a coffee cup on a hard-tiled floor and watched the cup explode into shards spreading to every corner of the room. I didn't know how I was going to support them through this. I didn't know how they were going to react to seeing us again. In many ways, I felt as though I had failed them. I had promised them a new sibling. We had dreamed about him together, and made plans about what we were going to do with him and what we would teach him. Now, all those plans and dreams lay there, shattered across the floor.

As we pulled up the driveway and put the vehicle in park, the kids ran up to us for hugs and kisses. Carson, almost 6, started crying the moment he saw us. Zoey, only 2.5 years old, was just happy to see us again. As we held them close, it felt like they were the potter that entered the room and carefully and lovingly picked up the pieces of that shattered coffee cup spread across the room, applied adhesive to each piece with great care, and slowly put that coffee cup together again. I felt my strength returning because I could feel that they had forgiven me for any failures around their brother, and I knew their love was there holding me up.

Yes, as a parent, you want to be strong for your children, and sometimes, if you're willing, those same children will give you the courage to be strong for them. Without them, I'm not sure how the rest of that day would have been. Not only did they pour out their love on us, but they also provided some much-needed comic relief to the whole group. After all, all their favourite uncles and aunts were in the same room. The kids barely knew whom to talk to because each person in that room was extremely special to them.

I wandered around the house, unable to sit still for more than a few minutes. I barely ate; actually, I realized that I had barely eaten at all that day. Hunger just didn't exist; my body was fighting so hard to simply make it through that there was no time for hunger. It all felt like a dream. Time flew by at warp speed, all the while standing completely still. It was like trying to focus on a specific detail on the side of the road as you were flying down the highway.

At last, it came time to leave. "Me come home?" Zoey asked. My eyes started to well. "No, sweetheart, you and your brother get to sleep at Beppe and Grandpa's tonight; mommy and daddy are going to go home and try and get some sleep too, but don't worry, we'll see you in the morning...at the... cemetery."

We didn't get the chance to sing the kids their bedtime prayers that night. We said goodnight, gave them kisses and hugs, and promised them over and over that we would see them the next day. We talked about their baby brother, how he wasn't coming home with us, but that he was going to live with Jesus, and how we were going to be burying his body in the ground the next day. We told them that their baby brother had died, but his spirit would go to live with Jesus and watch down on our family.

How do you tell your kids that the baby growing in mommy's tummy for the last nine months is no longer coming to join our family here on earth? How do you explain that to a child when you struggle to understand and accept it yourself?

"Goodnight, my little buddy. Goodnight, my little girl. Get some rest, and we'll see you tomorrow."

What do you wear to your child's funeral? I stood there in front of my closet. No, Ezra wouldn't like this one...no; that's too dark...no; that's not dressy enough. *I guess this will do,* I thought; *Ezra would have liked this.* I put on my dress shirt, pants, and funky asteroid socks. With the kids still at my in-laws, getting ready for the worst day of my life made it a little easier.

I had been to a few funerals before, my grandfather, great-grandparents, and friends' siblings and relatives, but this one was different. All those people had lived their lives, or at least a portion of it. They had the chance to see the trees swaying in the wind, the water lapping onto the shore, and the flowers blooming in springtime. They had the opportunity to make and lose friends, taste delicious food, and have other grand and mundane experiences.

They had the chance to be a brother, a son, a mother, a cousin, and a grandparent. Ezra had none of those things. He never got to experience the world and meet all the people who would love him. Other funerals had a mixture of sadness, happiness, and legacy. Other funerals had family and friends walk up to a microphone and speak a few words about the deceased's impact on their lives. This one would be different, though. What would we say about Ezra, the baby who didn't get the chance to take a breath?

Between sobs, we got ready. I called the funeral director to ensure they had some chairs for our grandparents. Even amid my grief, it was still in my nature to make sure others were being cared for. I couldn't help it; my parents had engrained it into my DNA.

It's been a pattern in my life to look out for others and then to look out for myself. Over the course of our relationship, this had caused a strain on Gina and me, especially early on. "Why are you helping out these other people when we need you here right now?" she would say. I never had a good answer for her. *That's just the way I'm wired,* I thought.

The plan was set for the funeral. We'd go to the cemetery, have the service, and then everyone would head back to my in-laws' farm to have a few beers and some food. My phone buzzed. "Hey...would you be okay if we brought our kids to the farm afterward? We're having trouble finding a babysitter for the whole afternoon, and we want to be there for you guys," read the text message. *That's a great idea,* I thought; *the kids will need that distraction.* I texted a few other friends that were going to be there and encouraged them to bring their kids afterward as well. At least our kids would see their friends and hopefully would provide some distraction for a little while.

Shortly after 10:00 a.m. that Sunday morning, Gina and I got in the van, the base of the baby seat still installed, and drove to the cemetery. We pulled in, and the driveway was already lined with the cars of everyone we considered family. We parked and just sat there, physically unable to move. We didn't get out of the van; we couldn't. The funeral director saw us and waved for us to follow him in our vehicle. We weaved through the cemetery, following the hearse on the way to the graveside, where we would tuck in our child for the last time.

A tiny white box stood atop a little hole. A small pile of dirt was off to the side of the hole. The sun was out and not too warm; the wind was blowing nicely, cooling us off that August day. The funeral director opened the little casket, and there lay our little boy. He was dressed in a white shirt and swaddled in an Elmo blanket. He looked so peaceful as if he was just having a nap. I looked up around us; gravestones lined the other side of the road. The shimmering green grass stretched out behind and beside us. To the left of us, in the distance, was the tree line, big trees that stood over the boundary of the cemetery, guarding all those that lay there within the cemetery limits. I could hear the birds chirping from their perches in the trees, singing a song that strangely comforted me. It sounded like an army of angels singing their songs of praise about their newest recruit in heaven, a little boy who would make them laugh, bring tears to their eyes with little side comments, and give them kisses and hugs.

"We're ready," Gina and I told the funeral director. He closed the casket, disappeared in the hearse, then returned with a convoy of trucks and cars. The kids saw us sitting beside the casket and bolted toward us. Carson, never backing down from a challenge and always making his own obstacle course, saw the casket and decided it would be a good idea to use it as a hurdle. As he sprinted towards us, I could see what was going through his mind. I held my breath and watched him soar over the little white box, take a step, and wrap his arms around Gina. *Holy crap*, I thought, *that could have been bad.*

We sat with our two living children right in the front. Surrounding us was our family and close friends. The pastor began the ceremony. "Dearly beloved, we are gathered here..." Tears flowed, noses sniffed, and people leaned against each other to stay standing so they wouldn't crumple into the grass, breaking down in their emotions. The kids each laid a white rose on the little white box. As our little family sat there, we were finally all together. Two adults and two kids sitting in chairs, and one lying in a little casket. All together, for the first and last time. As we sat there listening to the words of the pastor, feeling the support of those around us, Carson began to rub Gina's back and mine gently and soothingly. Comforting us as we held him as closely as we could between us. His touch seemingly said, "We're in this together... we're in this together forever."

Then they lowered Ezra into the earth.

Grief-stricken, and tear-stained, we collectively sang the doxology which will forever take on a new meaning:

Praise God from who all blessings flow,
Praise him all creatures here below,
Praise him above ye heavenly host,
Praise Father, Son, and Holy Ghost.
Amen.

The grave crew came and started to fill the hole that now possessed our baby boy. "You are all welcome to join us at the farm right now; please feel free to leave here whenever you would like," I somehow squeaked out. But nobody moved. We all watched the crew take out their shovels, put it into the pile of dirt on the grass, and scoop each shovel into the hole. I couldn't take my eyes off the shovel as it filled itself with dirt, pivoted slightly, and released the dirt into the hole in the ground. There was something comforting in it as well.

When my grandfather died, the pile of dirt beside the grave looked like a mountain compared to this pile. After they had lowered my grandfather into the ground, each person took a turn grabbing the shovel, piercing the dirt pile to fill up the shovel, and released the dirt into the ground. I can still hear the sound of the dirt hitting the casket. It feels a little morbid to do something like that, and yet, there's comfort in taking care of your own until the very end.

Maybe it's a first-born thing. I'm the oldest of four children and was raised to care for my own. So watch out for those around you, family or close friends. It's the code. It's the way it is. It's what you do.

The funeral director whispered in my ear, "If you would like, you are welcome to scoop some dirt into the ground." I just couldn't do it. I wanted to, but I couldn't move. I felt paralyzed.

When the hole was filled, they took the patch of grass that had been removed and lovingly tamped it back into its spot in the earth, tucking my son into his forever resting place. When the man started patting the grass with his tamper, I almost shouted. I almost got up, pushed him aside, and tucked him in myself. But I still couldn't move. My legs were stuck where they were planted. So, there I sat, watching this man I didn't know, tuck my son into the ground. I looked away for a brief moment, scanning the faces of the people around me, all eyes fixated on this man tamping the ground. When I looked back, the man took on a glow. He was an angel, taking all the care and love of the world, facilitating us to say goodbye while the angels in the trees were throwing a party welcoming our son to their family.

Gina and I made our way back to the farm. As we pulled up the long driveway, I saw Carson sitting on a patch of grass on the side of the driveway up by the house. I parked the car and Gina, and I went to sit beside him. "Are you okay, buddy?" I asked.

"Yeah," he said, "I'm just sitting here waiting for my friends to come."

"You hungry at all? We got some food inside," I said.

No," he said, staring down the driveway, "I'm just going to sit here for a while and think."

"Do you mind if we sit here for a little while with you?

"Yeah, that would be good."

So there we sat, looking down the driveway. Waiting. Waiting for some sort of chariot to come flying down the driveway with our other son. We sat there in silence. There was nothing to say.

"You guys never listen to me." My son's words pierced the silence.

"Uh...what do you mean, buddy?" Gina said.

"Well, all this time, I've been telling you that he was going to be a boy! You guys never listen!" he said as his lips slowly curled into a proud, big brother smile. The corners of my lips turned into a big smile as tears started streaming down my face.

"Ha, I guess you're right, buddy...we should listen to more of your instincts," I said as my eyes met his, beaming as only a proud father could. Our eyes held there for a while, exchanging meaning. *How I wish I could fix this for you, buddy...I hope you know how much I love you, and I will always be right here by your side whenever you need it. We're in this together, and I'm going to do my best to support you in whatever way you'll let me* I said through my eyes.

I know, dad, his eyes said, *I know. And I love you, and my whole family. Especially my little brother Ezra.*

Without a word, we were wrapped in a love so deep, a love that I had never experienced before. A love that reached down from one heart into another. Crying, grief-stricken, in absolute pain, while also delighting in the vulnerability, joy, and feeling of togetherness at the same time; it was pure love.

That afternoon was a blur. We laughed together; we cried together; we drank, and broke bread together. We watched the army of children run around together, playing as if it was any other Sunday. Screams of delight and fights, ran through the acres of farm that spread out over the countryside. It was a community. A community of broken-hearted, love-filled individuals brought together through a devastating, life-altering experience. And out of that painful, heart-wrenching experience, a new love poured out for one another.

That night we took our two living children home while our third lay in the ground, watching over us. I wondered if Ezra was sitting there watching us get in the van to make the short trek home. I wondered what he was thinking. I wondered what God was whispering in his ear as he met the folks he was surrounded with in heaven.

That night we held our kids tight, kissing them, hugging them, covering them in our tears and us in theirs. Tears of loss, tears of love, and tears of hope. As each child lay in their beds, we gently patted the sheets around them, tucking them securely into their beds, and we sang:

> *Now I lay me down to sleep*
> *I pray the Lord my soul to keep.*
> *Guide me through the starry night*
> *And wake me when the sun shines bright.*
> *Now I lay me down to sleep*
> *I pray the Lord my soul to keep.*
> *If I die before I wake*
> *I pray the Lord my soul to take.*
> *Amen.*

That night, August 14, 2016, Gina and I sat on the couch after the kids had drifted off to sleep, having a drink. I opened Facebook and started to scroll through my feed. I clicked on the "What's on your mind, Jason?" button and started to write: "Today we laid to rest our baby Ezra William. He was born into God's hands on August 12th at 3:46 p.m. weighing 7lbs 4 ozs, and was 21 1/2 inches long. Although he was beautiful, and this is the hardest thing we have ever done, he has blessed our lives richly. We appreciate your thoughts and prayers as we move forward as a family."

I looked over at Gina, "Can I post this? Are you ready for this?"

"I don't know if I'll ever be ready," she said through tears, "but this is our new reality." She reached over and hit the publish button. I closed the computer right away, not wanting to look at what was going to happen. My phone started to light up. Facebook messages and comments, text messages, and phone calls started to pour in. I put my phone on silent and sat there sipping my whiskey.

CHAPTER 3

It Takes a Community To Grieve

SEPTEMBER 2016

A few short weeks later, Gina and I sat in the living room drinking coffee, surrounded by cards and flowers. Oh my, the flowers. Gina and I talked about opening our own flower shop because of the sheer number of flowers we received. There were flowers in the kitchen, in the dining room, and even in the bathrooms. It turned into a routine with the flower shop. Each day the florist, John, would call to make sure we'd be home that morning. He'd show up with his little pug dog sitting in the front seat; some days, the dog was dressed with little dog-sized pilot goggles. He'd pull into the driveway and check in on us. "Hey guys, I'm here again; how are you guys doing today?"

"We're still here," I'd say. John would call us again later in the afternoon and drop off the next installment of flowers.

The flowers added some colour to our house and reminded us of the beauty that still existed in the world. After a few weeks, though, those flowers began to droop and turn brown, surrendering back into the ground from which they once came. These flowers, which had started out so beautiful, were almost a reminder that death is natural. A thing that should be expected. Let's face it; we are all going to die at some point. These flowers were a daily reminder that from death comes new life. The flowers droop and surrender back into the ground to nurture it before springing forward to new life once again.

As the flowers died, my conversation shifted with Gina from opening a flower shop to opening a Hallmark store with the amazing number of cards that we received. Cards from friends, extended family, church family, and complete strangers began to fill our house, and we meticulously placed each one with love and care throughout the house.

Each card struck different nerves. Some wrote a heartfelt speech, others talked about their own experience of having a stillbirth or miscarriage, and still, others quoted scripture and poems. I wrote down each verse and poem in my journal.

"The Lord is close to the broken-hearted and saves those who are crushed in spirit" (Psalm 34:18).

"Praise be to the God and Father of our Lord Jesus Christ, the Father of compassion and the God of all comfort, who comforts us in all our troubles so that we can comfort those in any trouble with the comfort we ourselves have received from God. For just as the sufferings of Christ flow over into our lives so also through Christ our comfort overflows. If we are distressed, it is for your comfort and salvation; if we are comforted, it is for your comfort, which produces in you patient endurance of the same sufferings we suffer. And our hope for you is firm because we know that just as you share in our sufferings, so also you share in our comfort" (2 Corinthians 1:3-7).

"You keep track of all my sorrows. You have collected all my tears in your bottle. You have recorded each one in your book" (Psalm 56:8).

Scripture and poetry became an outlet for me. I scoured the internet for them and listened to grief playlists on Spotify. Different songs began to take on new meanings, and words and phrases began to play over and over in my mind.

The reality started to set in. We had three children, but only two of their voices filled our house. As the calls, messages, and drop-ins began to infiltrate our house, I became our public relations spokesperson. A routine started to settle in: our doorbell would ring, and Gina would retreat to our room. I would take a breath, centre myself, and answer the door giving the same speech: "Hi...thanks for dropping by...yes...we are shocked as well...thanks so much for coming."

One person who stopped by to drop off some flowers and a card was my colleague, Keith. Keith is one of the most intelligent men I know. He's lived all around the world and has more wisdom in his little finger than I think I will ever have in my whole body. "How are you doing, Jason?" Keith asked.

"Well, we're doing alright, all things considered. We're taking it pretty easy right now, but I'm sure I'll be back at work in the next couple of weeks."

Keith and I have worked together for about 7 years or so, but just a year ago, we partnered with two others to form a leadership and conflict trans-formation "super" group. We had all worked together for a number of years serving congregations in the consulting business, but all of us had our own practices with a focus on workplaces as well. After a number of discussions, we finally decided to pull the trigger and put all of our work under one roof. Following years of working as solo entrepreneurs and business owners, we formed an organization to further support each other and our clients.

"How are you really doing? How's Gina and the kids?" Keith said, cutting through my rehearsed speech.

"Shitty, Keith. It's been a little crazy around here, and it's definitely been a struggle. To tell you the truth, I haven't really been upset with God yet, but I have been a little frustrated, saying; What the fuck, God, quite a few times."

"Yeah, I get that. I'd be pretty frustrated, too, I imagine."

"It's such a weird and depressing feeling. For the last nine months, we've been sitting here getting all excited for this baby, making plans, getting our-selves ready to have three kids in the house, and now I don't even know what

I'm going to say to people when they ask me how many kids we have. I mean, I don't ever want to forget him."

"You know, I lived in South Africa for a while, and they did something interesting that I found really honouring. When someone would ask them how many kids they had, they would answer, we have three children, two living."

"Huh...I'm going to think more about that, Keith; thanks for that."

"If you ever need anything, call me," Keith said, "also, work-wise, take your time, and let me know if you need anything covered."

As Keith walked out the door, I could feel my Public Relations armour sitting down at my feet, leaving me vulnerable from even that short discussion. I quickly put my armour back on to address the next text message, phone call, and visitor.

A similar routine happened with our neighbours. Gina would hear a car door or activity in the front of the house and immediately retreat to the backyard or into the house to avoid sharing the news. Our neighbour, Bryce, came out of the house early that week, seeing me on the front lawn. "Soooo? I noticed your car was gone for a few days! Any exciting announcements to tell me?"

In the months previous, we'd told everyone we were having a baby. I mean, who doesn't? I told neighbours, clients, and complete strangers; even the gas station attendant in our town knew we were having a baby! When you have good news to share, it's difficult to contain it. It bubbles up inside you until you can't handle it anymore and then explodes out to anyone and everyone who will listen. Bryce was excited for us, and you could hear it in his voice; you could see it in his approach. This would be the first of many who would excitedly ask the question.

"Well, Bryce," I said, my voice lowering, "we had a son, but...but...he didn't make it. We're not sure what happened. There are few theories, but...he didn't make it through the labour."

"Oh, Jason," he said, tears filling his eyes. "I'm so sorry; I don't know what to say..."

"There's really nothing to say, Bryce. It sucks."

As Bryce and I sat there talking, my work training kicked in. I slowly exited my body, flew up in the air, and watched the conversation happening below me. I was still fully present, feeling all my feelings but also hovering above me, feeling a dulled-down version of all the feelings. There I was, talking, sharing, connecting with another human being, all the while being detached from what I was saying. It's always a weird experience when it happens because you are fully there, present, in the conversation, connecting with the other person, feeling their feelings, and you're detached enough that those feelings aren't getting "the better of you." It's an out-of-body experience where you are watching yourself participate in a conversation as if it was someone else as if you were watching a movie. When watching an emotional film, you might cry a little, but you typically won't enter that stage of the "ugly cry." The one where you have no control over your emotions, when they simply take you over, and you can barely breathe. Your eyes become a river, and your nose immediately fills and plugs the nostrils as you sit there gasping for air.

I learned this idea of "rational detachment" from working with individuals in difficult situations. I first heard about it when I was working with individuals who were developmentally delayed. The question at that time was, "How can you connect with these individuals, empathize with them, but not take on their struggles?" This idea of rational detachment became increasingly important as I left the social service field and started my own business in conflict management. When I got my start, I was working with families that were going through separations and divorces and eventually moved my business into working with organizations and churches in conflict and leadership situations. For over ten years, I had been practicing this idea of rational detachment, and today talking with Bryce, I started to see that it would potentially be a helpful skill in the coming weeks and months.

As Bryce and I sat there talking on our front lawn, Carson skipped into the conversation, looked at the tears streaking my face and the ones streaming down Bryce's face, and said, very matter-of-factly, "My brother's dead."

He gave a half-smile, half-grief-stricken look, skipped off down the driveway, hopped on his bike, and started going up and down the sidewalk.

Hearing those words hurt me to the very core. It made it sound so final, so forever. We weren't really sure what to say to our kids when Ezra was delivered. Did we tell them that he went to be with Jesus? Did we tell them that he is forever sleeping? We wanted to make sure that they knew Ezra wasn't going to come strolling through the doors one day, so something about both of those sayings just didn't resonate with us. So, we told them that Ezra had died.

He was dead.

We told them that Ezra went to hang out with God and that we wouldn't be taking Ezra home with us because he was not alive. Zoey was too young to understand everything happening, but Carson? At that age, he had a pretty good understanding of what was happening. So was it a good decision? I suppose we'd probably never know until we're neck-deep in counseling fees.

Late that afternoon, the door opened, because only strangers rang our doorbell. It was our close friend, Amy, dropping off a hot meal for supper that evening. She approached me just after the funeral and said, "I'm going to call our friends and church family and set up meals for the next couple of weeks." There was no question in there; this was what would happen.

"That's alright, Amy, we'll be fine, and besides, I think cooking will be a nice distraction," I had initially told her. Instead, she just looked at me with a soft smile. "Sounds good, Jason, then you can cook breakfast and lunch, and I'll get people to take care of supper for you." Amy has this amazing thing about her; she knows what you need even when you don't know what you need, and you don't argue with her.

When Amy showed up with our first meal, it was already 5:00 p.m., and the thought of food hadn't even registered in my brain yet. *Dammit,* I thought *she was right! Even though I'm not hungry or thinking of food, these kids should probably have something.*

Gina and I both come from Dutch backgrounds. Her mom immigrated directly from Holland, and Gina's father and my parents were born here in Canada to Dutch immigrants. Apparently, Dutch Canadians are emotional eaters. Something remarkable happens in your life? A Dutch person will swing by your home with a freezer meal. Something devastating happens in your life? A Dutch person is going to swing by your house with a freezer meal and likely a hot meal, all wrapped in tea towels, ready to be served.

Apparently, the more devastated they think you might be, the more food they bring. People brought us supper for the next two-and-a-half weeks every evening around 5:00 p.m. Those were just the people that were organized. Others still, from various corners of our community, came by with freezer meals. It wasn't long until our chest freezer was full of meals.

The next evening, Gina and I were sitting with the kids watching some TV before starting the "get back in your room" bedtime routine, when we heard a faint knock on the door. Before we could even get up to see who it was, two people walked up our stairs, past the barking dog, and into the living room where we were sitting. "Hey guys, we were just thinking about you today and passing by your house and just felt like you could use a quick hug." They gave their hugs and not even two minutes later they were back in the car and out of the driveway. Gina and I looked at each other and couldn't stop smiling.

It was after this week that I started calling Ezra our "Devastating Blessing." I was ripped to shreds, and yet, through the pain, suffering, and grief, Gina and I had started to see the impact that our little Ezra was beginning to have on us and those around us. His life was short, just nine months in the womb, and already he had started to have an impact on us and those around us.

Ezra's legacy/message/lessons/impact was just beginning, but I began to see it in many different areas of my life. One of the clear correlations was related to the work I had been doing with congregations and businesses over the past number of years, specifically some of the church clients I had in the past year. I had been working around a renewal process with these churches that our organization facilitates. The process at its root is leading groups through three phases: Allowing for God, Listening for God, and Living for God.

Allowing for God is really around taking stock of our current reality — who are we, beauty, warts, and all - and then surrendering that reality over to God. In other words, what does it look like to surrender mind, body, and our soul to God? — not seeing our current reality as good or bad, but rather, what is. And offering that current reality, or surrendering that reality, over to God.

Then it's a matter of forming the specific questions that the congregation is seeking discernment on and entering into a time of listening for God, a time of basking in God's wisdom and presence. Then, we find ways to be still in the busyness, genuinely listen, and open ourselves to encounter God for what God has to say.

Then finally, coming together as a community, we listen for what we have all experienced God saying to us, and put a plan together so that we can live into where we feel God is calling us.

Through this work, I have witnessed communities struggle with what to do with their grief, their loss, and their suffering, especially in that first stage of surrendering or making space for God. Most of us are walking around with broken hearts. I know I've been broken-hearted many times in life; the time I didn't get selected for the soccer team, the girlfriend that broke up with me when a friend chose to hang out with another friend without me. I was broken-hearted when I lost my motorcycle in an accident, when my grandfather passed away, when my brother-in-law almost died in an accident, and even when my son got rejected by a friend at school. We all go through times when we feel a sense of being heartbroken. Churches and organizations are no different.

I started to see that some of the questions I had asked those churches were also questions I could turn on myself. Questions like, how do we hold the loss that we've experienced? For churches, how do we hold the loss we felt when members had left us? When we fired a staff member? When we didn't welcome someone different than us? How do we hold the loss that we grieve from past conflicts that have caused such tensions that we are still feeling them?

How do we sit with these sufferings and offer them up to God so we can enter into a time of transformation? How do we see the gift that loss has to offer us?

These last two questions were pivotal for me. How do I sit with this loss, the loss of my baby boy, and offer this experience to God so that I can enter into a time of transformation? Can I even see Ezra's delivery as a gift?

By the end of the week, I still didn't have an answer to those questions, and yet I couldn't help seeing the blessings that existed amongst the loss that we were experiencing. Losing Ezra fully ripped out my heart and also acted as a defibrillator. One that took my sedentary heart out and kick-started it back into pumping order.

In many ways, Ezra held up a mirror to me and said, "Is this really you? Is this who you have been called to be? Or did you get a little confused along the way?"

It takes a community to grieve a child, I thought. Yes, Gina and I were going to need each other, and we were both going to need others as well. There were certain things I wouldn't be able to understand because, well, I'm not a female. I would never be fully able to understand or know what it is like to lose a child from a female's perspective. Similarly, there would be things that Gina wouldn't be able to understand either because she's, well, not a male.

Gina and I sat outside as the moon took its place in the sky. I told Gina, "You have to promise me that you're not going to hole yourself up in your room. If that's the case, I'll get Amy, Melissa, and Ang on your case to take you out. Take you out for a drink, take you out to get your nails done, take you out so that you can see what the outside of our house looks like. I won't let you trap yourself in your room so that you're going through this on your own."

I knew her — after all, it had been fifteen years. I knew that in the face of adversity her "go-to actions" were to cut off the world, to take some time in the comfort of her own head to sort things out before re-emerging from her hiding place. She was kind of used to dealing with things by herself, after all;

she is a police officer. She routinely had to deal with tough situations on her own. I mean, she's a woman working in a man-dominated part of the world. She was often forced to deal with things on her own, and I knew this was something she would not be able to sort out on her own.

"Alright... deal," Gina said. "And that means you have to talk to me. You must tell me how you're doing even if you haven't figured it out already. You have to give me the raw emotions; tell me how your heart is." Gina cut right through me. *Yep,* I thought, *she just went straight to the core of what I do.* It's not that I don't share what's on my heart, but I spread it around a little. I test out little things here and there on different people within my community, but never anyone with the raw emotions. Different people get various excerpts as I analyze the heck out of what I think is going on. Then, once I've pieced it together, which typically takes less time than you think, I open my mouth and have a conversation with my wife about what's bothering me or what is going on for me. She knew she was about to be shut out, and she called me on it immediately.

"Deal," I said, "you have yourself a deal. So how are we actually going to put this into practice?"

"We're going to have nightly check-ins. Every night, we'll sit down, have a drink or some tea, and check in with one another."

"Alright," I said, "let's do it."

It takes a community to grieve a child, I thought. Gina and I needed each other more than we ever needed. And neither of us needed our masked selves, the self that we'd been walking around with every day that was there to protect ourselves. No, we needed to be our true selves, the vulnerable self, the self pointing itself towards Creator, the self that is who we were created to be. It's almost as if, at that exact moment, the scales fell from our eyes, and we were actually able to see who each other was. It wasn't the masked selves that we had put up over the years. Those things that protect us from making us vulnerable, from making us real. Those masks we put up to hide our genuine emotions because we don't like those emotions or we have a hard time figuring out what to call them. Those masks we put up so that we can avoid some of those conversations that are a little more awkward.

Gina and I had a couple of subjects that we could talk about, but not really talk about. So was a little awkward. We had learned how to have conversations about sex, religion, and our deepest innermost wants and needs in a very controlled conversation. But not one where we could really express our desires or needs. That week we discussed stuff we had never discussed in our fifteen years together. Not because we hadn't wanted to, but because it wasn't completely safe to talk about. However, this new commitment to sharing what was on each other's hearts dislodged all the stuff blocking us from taking our relationship and conversations to that next level.

I hadn't actually started my own grief journey yet, either. I had to ensure everyone else was on their way before I could explore my grief. Gina gave me permission to begin that journey, and I knew that I was not going to be able to do it all myself. I have always loved to be in community. Call it extroversion, call it being outgoing, call it whatever you want, but from a young age, I loved being around people. When I was a child, my mom would take me along grocery shopping. I loved going grocery shopping, rows and rows of treats, and I would get to pick a couple of treats for our snacks and lunches. The best part about grocery shopping for me, though? It was all the different people we would be around. I used to walk up to people, ask them how they were doing, and then invite them to sleep over at my house for three nights. I'm not sure why three nights, but it seems like it's just enough to really get to know another person, doesn't it?

Growing up, I would always get in trouble for randomly bringing friends home unannounced just before supper time. "We're not going to have enough food, Jason! I wasn't prepared to have more mouths here for supper; you have to tell me these things!" Mom was probably right, but I'm not really sure how I would have told her; we didn't exactly have cell phones to make those calls yet.

All throughout my life, I have had amazing people surrounding me. Especially as Gina and I began our life together and started having children, there were a few people around us who we became really close with. Even though we knew we had a strong community, neither of us would have guessed the depth and strength our community had to give. During the first couple weeks after Ezra's delivery, friends would come over with tea and drinks just to sit there, cry, and laugh with us.

Every day Gina or I would get a call or a text from a friend that went something like this: "Hey...how's your day/week going?" or "Just wanted you to know we're thinking about you."

Every day that went past, we were forced to rely on our community. We could barely function ourselves, and depending on others was one of the most difficult things to do. Both Gina and I come from pretty proud backgrounds. Proud in the sense that our ancestors worked their asses off to provide for their families. They did a lot for themselves and for their community. They set up churches, schools, cared for each other's kids, and helped each other out. They looked out for each other, and it felt like that was something that was passed down to me.

It not only has been passed down to me but it has also been ingrained into my life in many ways. It's one of the reasons I do the work that I do; it's one of the reasons I started my working life in social services; it's one of the reasons I was fascinated by psychology and sociology in university. It's been ingrained in me that if you see someone needing help, you go over to them and help them out. If you see a need in a community, you work towards fulfilling it. If you see someone struggling, you see what you can do to help them. You always start by asking, and if they say no, you talk to others who might be closer to them to ensure that person is supported.

But to accept help from people when it's offered? That's an entirely different animal. It feels awkward, strange, and weird for me to accept help, especially when I know I'm capable of doing what is being offered. I have asked people for help a lot in my life, but that feels different. When we needed to build a pergola at our old house, I asked my handy friends to come and "help me" build it (if you call them doing all the work and me only providing them with the appropriate materials and the occasional witty remark "helping me"). If I'm running late and need someone to help me out with the kids, I don't have any problems asking a friend to help.

But there's something different about people coming up to you and saying, "Hey, I want to come and help you, whether it's cooking you some food, cleaning your house, taking your kids out for a bit, whatever it is, I'm here to help you." It's weird, awkward, and it's uncomfortable to say, "Yes, please come over and clean my house while my wife and I lie in bed quietly sobbing." Because it's something you should be able to do yourself, and when the grief hits, it feels hard even to get dressed. There's also something vulnerable about accepting help, there's something that makes you feel exposed, stripped naked, and it can feel dangerous.

Keep going; we don't stop. This sentence could have been my mantra growing up. Keep going; we don't stop. It has surrounded me since I was a little kid. The doctor might tell you to walk it off if you get hurt. If you were tired, your coach would tell you to dig in and keep going. If you wanted to take a day off work, your parents would laugh and tell you to get your ass in the car. You have got to hustle more, you've got to stay busy, and you've got to dig deeper. *Work hard, play hard* was the saying my friends and I repeatedly heard and said. We worked our asses off, and we played the same way. We don't slow down; we keep going, and we don't stop.

This saying has certainly served me well over the years. It taught me the value of hard work. Since I was a young kid, I was working. My first job was working in a greenhouse around the age of 9. I worked on Saturdays, transplanting and planting flowers into flats full of dirt.

Once I was a few years older, I worked in the greenhouse all day, went home and took a shower, and then got picked up so that I could babysit kids in the evening. My first summer job was working on a farm for a minimum of ten hours a day. That first summer, I was putting in over fifty hours a week out in the fields regardless of the weather, tending to vegetables, picking vegetables, and packing vegetables. We keep going; we don't stop. Do you want a holiday or a day off? The vegetables don't stop growing, so get back to work! While each day wasn't necessarily fun, it definitely taught me the value of hard work, which has served me very well in my adult life.

Keep going; we don't stop. A few years ago, when Carson was 3 years old, I went on a bachelor-party ski trip for three days. I couldn't wait for the trip — a few days away with the guys; it was going to be great. We got to the ski resort, grabbed our skis, and went to the top of the hill. We coasted down, carving this way and that, feeling the wind in our faces. Once at the bottom, we went up again, this time to a larger part of the hill. A double black diamond. As I stood at the top of the hill, I swallowed hard. It had been a while since I had been on skis, but I was determined. After all, we face our fears, and we put them into submission, right? Well, not even a quarter of the way down the hill, I turned to carve left, hit a patch of ice, slid, and then caught some snow.

Wham!

My shoulder went right into the hard, packed snow, and I could hear a pop while pain filled my body. I had fractured my collarbone. Day one, run two on a three-day ski trip, and I was confined to the hot tub for the next few days.

When I got home, I was pretty useless. It was difficult for me to change diapers or even help Gina out around the house. She offered to get me some help, family and friends, to come in and help around the house and with the kids while she was off at work. I refused. After all, we keep going; we don't stop.

Several days later, I was trying to get my son into the car so that I could bring him to daycare and go to work. As we exited the house and walked to the car, Carson escaped. He took off down the driveway and started to head towards the busy corner we were close to. I took off after him, got to the end of the driveway, and turned to go down the sidewalk after Carson. Only, I hit the patch of ice, and my feet turned towards the sky as I came down on my shoulder. The one that was put into a sling only four days before.

So, you know what I did? I picked myself off the sidewalk, wiped off the tears, got my son in the car, and brought him to daycare. I drove myself to work, where they told me I should go to the hospital. So, I drove myself to the hospital. Do you know why? We keep going; we don't stop.

In the past ten years, our little family has experienced some pretty crazy things. Both my dad's and my father-in-law's barns burnt down; we've experienced breast cancer, punctured pancreas, rare heart conditions, and motorcycle accidents, to list a few. Throughout it all, we kept going. We did not stop. We got up each morning, put on our armour, laced up our shit-kicking boots, rallied together, and gave our best battle cry. We did not stop. We got fierce. Nothing would stand in our way of figuring out how to house thousands of chickens that were coming in a few weeks. Nothing would stop us through the cancer treatments or supporting a brother in pain. We would be relentless walking beside the doctors as they tried to figure out the right medication treatment plan to attack a nasty heart condition. These things, these conditions, experiences, set backs, are only temporary. We can work through them. We can stand up to them.

We fight with every fiber in our body against whatever holds us back. We become a puzzle-master, searching for the right piece to fall in place, and when it doesn't fit, we grab a knife and start hacking away at the piece to force it into place. It's the ultimate tough-mudder obstacle course. We give all blood, sweat, and tears to the obstacles put down in front of us as we search for the finish line. We go over them, we go around them, and when there is no other way, we go right fucking through.

We keep going; we don't stop. This mantra, this motto, this sentence has served me for my whole life. Time and time again, it has proven itself worthy of a slogan to plaque and hang on the wall. It has enabled me to get to where I am today in my relationships with family, friends, my work, and business. It's the hustle; it's the grind; it's what you do.

And it's completely flawed.

When we lost Ezra, my sister-in-law said something profound. "Throughout everything, we have fought and succeeded, but we couldn't have stopped or fixed this." It hit me at that moment. This is not a problem to solve; this is not a conflict to resolve; this is a tension to navigate. So, yes, we will keep going. We will fight to learn from this devastating blessing. We will fight to grow. We will wake up every morning, put on our brave face and give our best warrior cry. But...but...we will stop...because we can't keep going until we stop. We cannot keep going the way that we did previously.

I'm tired.

I'm tired of blowing past every incident or experience in life as a passing thought. Not dwelling in the learning, dwelling in the experience. I'm tired of always hustling on work and not hustling on my family. I'm done with grazing the surface of experiences without looking at what lies beneath. I'm done with hustling for the sake of hustling so that I can "keep up" with the world. I cannot stop everything. I could do everything completely perfectly, and something rotten could still happen. You cannot fix everything. You can read every do-it-yourself book and watch every YouTube video, and that thing you're trying to fix? It will remain shattered.

Here's the biggest learning of all. This mantra of keep going, we don't stop, is too easy. It's too easy to put your head down and not stop. It's easy to swoop in and provide a solution. It's easier to keep going and not stop because we never have to face what's happening within us. We don't have to stop and face those emotions. We don't have to stop and address the injustice. We don't have to stop so that we can address the pain and suffering, or the wrong that has been caused. We just keep going, we don't stop, and we don't address the discomfort.

That's why stopping actually takes courage—stopping to enter the pain of another and taking the time to join the shit-storm when you can't even see three feet in front of you—sitting in the shame, grief, and fear of your inner self and sorting through your stuff, picking it up, looking it over, and taking one step forward in an attempt to be better. That takes some courage. That takes some bravery. That is the actual work of the warrior.

The crux of the warrior is their ability to go when they need to go and the knowledge or discernment to stop when they need to stop. The work of the warrior is never-ending. There is no finish line, per se, but rather a continuous learning experience. Through every experience, a warrior will wade into the waters and sit with the discomfort. They will go out in the storm instead of taking comfort in their own home when things get uncomfortable. They will get their ass kicked over and over, and at the end of every ass-kicking, they rise to their feet, look their opponent in the eye, and ready themselves to fight again.

That's where they don't stop. That's where they are relentless.

They always get back up, but they know the difference between struggling to get back on their feet and learning what knocked them down in the first place.

They don't aimlessly take an ass-whipping and go on the attack again. No, they learn from their opponent; they learn from their mistakes, and the things they encounter in their lives. They take in what is happening around them, the good and the bad. They're willing to sit in the pause with others and help them on their journey. They are the people who will always have your back.

Then one weekend, I began to write. A friend's parents offered us their cottage to use for a weekend in September, and we humbly accept their invitation.

We drive the three-and-a-half hours to the middle of nowhere to a little cottage that overlooks the lake. The place is beautiful. The cottage has three tiny little bedrooms, a bathroom, and a kitchen/living room that opens to the deck. The floors squeak with each step you take, and the furniture looks like it has existed for at least fifty years. On the left side of the property lay a bunkhouse. A little home that consisted of one big room with bunk beds and a queen-sized bed, with enough room to put up a pack-and-play or an air mattress. A little space to just sleep. I had never been to this place before, but something about it made me feel comfortable. Something that made me feel like I was home.

My mind went back to my youth, where we would drive, seemingly forever, up to my grandparents' cottage. Their cottage had a few extra sleeping areas, but other than the actual layout; the feelings were the same. Squeaky floors, old and tattered furniture, a fire pit outside, and a sitting area that looks over the lake. We would go up there with my aunts, uncles, and cousins to visit my grandparents, who always looked so comfortable, and in their element when they were at the cottage. We would sit there as a family. We would talk, play games, swim, and boat, catch fish, and enjoy nature. Something about being up at the cottage made me feel close to Creator.

As I sat on the porch sipping a coffee and watching the kids brave the cold water, I took in the familiar feeling of being "home," I couldn't help but see God all around me. He was in the trees waving in the wind; I could see her in the water that lapped up against the kids' feet as they screamed in delight. I saw him in the birds that sang in the trees and the loons that sang their beautiful song. It was at that moment that I knew I needed to write. I needed to get it out. I had been talking to Gina, and I had been talking to some friends, but I hadn't been talking to myself or God. I hadn't gotten it all out.

So, I started to write:

August 12, 2016, a Friday. That is a day I will never forget. That morning I got up just before the kids, just like every other day, put on a cup of coffee, and read my Bible. I don't remember what I read, but it was one of Paul's letters to the church—I think 2 Corinthians. After that, I fed the kiddos breakfast, oatmeal for Zoey, and cereal for Carson, read a bit more from one of my books, and then showered and got ready for work that day.

Today's "work" was attending day two of the Global Leadership Summit. Upon arrival, I snuggled into the back pew, readied my notebook to take some notes, and waited for my friend Andrew who was also at the Summit. A little later that morning, I texted back and forth with Gina, who told me that she was experiencing contractions as she watched the kids bike up and down the sidewalk. I immediately got excited and admittedly a little nervous. After all, we were about to have our third child. Wow, how life was going to change. I was nervous about when Gina would end maternity leave; I would have three kids to watch when she returned to work. Three kids ran in different directions, three kids to get ready to go out and three kids to feed and care for. But I was also excited about all of that. Another voice around the table, another child laughing and bugging their brother and sister, another child to nurture, care for, and to love.

The words and tears didn't stop coming. I sat there for an hour, crying, writing, blowing my nose, and drinking coffee. Every now and then, one of our children would come up to me and see if I wanted to play, but I couldn't tear myself away from the words. Finally, I shifted from my words to the words of the book I was reading, *Love Warrior* by Glennon Doyle Melton.

While the book didn't stop my tears, it made me realize I wasn't alone. Glennon seemingly told me on multiple pages, "You are not alone, Jason, and that pain you feel? It's real. Feel it; go ahead; I'll be right here with you. I'll sit with you in your discomfort, sit here in your grief, and won't rob you of it." I wrestled with the book, pushed back, and couldn't stop reading. Then Glennon said to me:

> Grief is love's souvenir. It's our proof that we once loved. Grief is the receipt we wave in the air that says to the world: *Look! Love was once mine. I loved well. Here is my proof that I paid the price.*

I put the book down, and I smiled through my tears. Yes, it was time to stop and appreciate my souvenir. I could not keep going anymore; it was time to dwell within the gift that was given and explore what love meant. Explore the depths that love had to offer. Explore the side of love that we don't talk about enough. I could feel Ezra in that moment saying to me, "Just be Dad, sit down, enjoy me, enjoy your other children, dwell on me for a while because I come bearing gifts."

Writing used to be a huge part of my life. It started in my later years of high school when I was in a band. I was the one that played rhythm guitar but had a deep love for words and poetry. Jim Morrison was one of my poetic heroes, the way he could connect words with images and make them come alive. So I started writing lyrics for songs, writing poetry, and even trying a short story once. I took some Creative Writing courses in high school and began to dabble in the writing field. Several years later, in University, I would often find myself outside the Starbucks that employed me, with a notepad and a pen, writing prose and poetry on my breaks. Watching the hustle and bustle of people whipping in and out in search of their daily caffeine fix. I would sit there and write what was happening inside of me: my thoughts, my fears, my desires, and my experiences.

When I started my conflict management business, I continued writing, but in a different capacity. I started writing blogs about relationships, communication, conflict, and leadership transformation. I didn't realize it at the time, but something inside me was missing. I was still writing and communicating, but I was no longer deeply in touch with who I was or what was happening inside me. I was no longer writing to process what was going on for me, but I was trying to help others through my writing. As a result, I slowly lost touch with how to express my thoughts and what was happening inside me.

It wasn't until I was on a work retreat, where we intentionally, as a group, spent some time in silence and reflection, that I got a taste of what I was missing.

We all had an hour to sit, reflect, write, read, meditate, or nap. So, I sat there and wrote. I wrote a poem. A poem about love, a poem about my search for it, a poem that said:

Love, she's a funny thing
She never gives up
When times get rough
She waits until you're ready

Love, she's a tough thing
She'll take a punch
And get back up
And never look away

Love, she's a selfless thing
She'll cleanse your cup
And fill you up
Never to ask for payment

Love, she's a beautiful thing
She's a night sky
At a sunrise
Her rays are ever shining

Love, she's a restoring thing
She sees my faults and
Doesn't care at all
She wraps herself around me.

Love, she's a picturesque thing
She'll look at you

And all will fade
Her beauty is so blinding

Love, she's a brave thing
She'll take a risk
Even if
There's no net when she's falling

Love, she's a Godly thing
She'll never stop
When I screw up
She'll hold me close and steady

Love, she's a patient thing
She'll always wait
When I am late
She never will forsake me

Love, she's a funny thing
She holds me up
When I can not
She works forever in me.

Love is a verb thing
She always runs
She's never done
She'll never be caught sleeping.

After that day, I started to realize what was missing in my life, but I couldn't figure out what to do with it. My to-do list, client list, family, friends, and church took up most of my time, and I didn't think I could fit anything else into it. I wanted to go to the gym more, spend more time in devotions, and go on more dates with my wife, but where was I going to fit it all in? So, I did what most people did: I ignored the feeling and continued with the busyness. The chaotic, disordered busyness.

At the beginning of 2016, I could feel that my wife and I weren't as connected as we had been in the past. We had been married for almost nine years, so I thought maybe things were just getting stale. So my New Year's resolution for the start of 2016 was to date my wife. I sat down with Gina and said to her, "Let's do something different this year; once a month, let's go out with just the two of us. Let's have a monthly date night, get away from the kids, get a babysitter, and go and do something with just the two of us."

"Sure," Gina said, "we can do that if you want."

It took us about a week and a half to figure out an evening that would work for both of our schedules. Gina was working full-time doing shift work, and I worked whenever Gina was home. It was great for the kids; they only had to be shipped off to daycare about five to six days a month, but for the two of us? There wasn't much time left. We agreed to alternate the planning, so one month, I would plan what we were going to do, and the next month Gina would do the planning.

We made it four months before the whole idea fell to the periphery. Gina pushed off our date night one month and said we would do it the month following, but it never happened. I could feel us growing distant, but I didn't know what the problem was.

When Ezra was delivered, we started talking again. It kick-started our relationship again. Then we did counseling and realized something together; all those things—the task lists, our work lives, our family lives, our social lives—came before our relationship. We prioritized everything else before our relationship and each of us individually.

My priorities had become so jumbled that it was hard to tell where to start.

My work life had slowly crept to the top of my priority list. Years of self-employment, working around the clock and thinking about business all the time had gradually taken over my life. I had started to idolize the word "hustle," making it my mantra for life. Everything was about hustling. Hustling from one appointment to the next. One meeting to the next. One client to the next. I was always thinking about what could be improved in my business and how to approach different situations that my clients were facing. I was proud that I was responding to clients' emails until midnight and then again at 6:00 a.m. the following morning. It was the hustle; it was the life.

Only it wasn't. I could see that my relationship with my kids was starting to suffer. Even though I was at home with them for much of the week, caring for them, cooking them supper, and ensuring they got their baths, I wasn't making them a priority. Instead, I fit them in between meetings, report writing, and client conversations. Although the kids were a verbal close second on the priority list, they really didn't compete with work. And Gina and I? Well, we made time when all those other things gave us an opportunity.

Oh, and focus on me? Yeah, that wasn't happening. I would do things to grow professionally to learn new skills, tips, and tricks that would help me in my job, but I wasn't spending much time actually working on being a better me.

One of Ezra's gifts to me was boldly saying, "Hey! You're saying one thing and doing another. Get your shit together!" It was a message I could finally hear.

I knew that re-prioritizing my life would take some work, and I realized I needed to start writing again. I needed a place to process my thoughts, talk about the other areas of my life outside of work, and talk about my learnings and screw-ups. Writing had always been a way of processing; it had been years since I had written anything personal.

I had been thinking about a parenting blog in the back of my mind. I already had two kids who had significantly impacted my life and gave me countless stories, and I knew there weren't many male perspectives when it came to parenting.

Sure, there were dad blogs that talked about the latest cars, where all the hot fishing spots were, and the coolest technology that was coming out. But something was missing from all those places. A male voice around the stresses and joys of being a dad, a male voice around men's insecurities, a male voice that didn't seem to exist in many places.

It wasn't until I was sitting outside with my dad, chatting about life's most significant problems a few months after Ezra's delivery, that I realized I would start a blog. So we sat there, a few drinks in already, when my dad started talking about what it means to be a male. "You know, Jason, I'm in this men's Bible study, and it's refreshing to hear these other guys' perspectives on things. I mean, we talk. We share stuff. I'm not sure I've ever discussed some of this stuff before."

It was at that moment that I knew I needed to start writing. Here was my dad, twenty-some years my elder, talking about how he's had all these things going on inside him, but didn't know where to put them. I had felt the same way; the only way I found to get them out was through writing. I didn't have any male influences to show me how to process these thoughts and get them out of me, and I knew I wasn't alone. So I decided to take a step in courage and start a blog.

It all started primarily selfishly. I knew that I had to do some writing to figure out all my thoughts and feelings. I knew that I had to put pen to paper to figure out what was really happening inside of me. So why not put them up for others to learn along with me? *Maybe they'll have similar struggles, and then we can talk together to figure out this thing called life,* I thought.

The following day I started throwing around blog names with Gina. "What about...All things Dad...or DadLife, or..." I started saying.

"Hmmm...sure...all good suggestions." She smiled sarcastically, "Or, what about They Call Me Dad."

They Call Me Dad. They Call Me Dad. We promised to sleep on it for a few nights before committing to anything.

Thankfully, when my business started, I learned how to make websites. Since then, I've had multiple iterations and have, as a result, spent a fair amount of time creating websites for myself. I like to think it's because I'm resourceful and that it's something I enjoy doing, but really, I'm Dutch and cheap. Finally, a couple of weeks later, I was ready to unveil my new site. I created my Facebook page, invited a couple of people, and started writing:

> Hey there and welcome to They Call Me Dad! This site is hosted by an imperfect dad, who deeply loves his kids and constantly screws up. I'm hoping you enjoy your stay here and that you'll come back often to see what we're up to. My hope with this blog is to share some insights into our little view of the world. All in all, I'm hoping that writing about fatherhood will not only help you in some way, shape or form, but it will also help me to be a better dad. I'm hoping it will help me to stay in the present, sort through some thoughts about what life is like being a father, husband, brother, and friend, and provide another avenue for me to deal with some of the grief that comes along with losing a baby.
>
> A couple of things you should probably know about me:
>
> - I have three fantastic kids – two are living
> - I am fortunate to be going through life with a wonderful friend and wife
> - I'm a follower of Christ who firmly believes in his grace and undying love
> - I love motorcycles and can't wait for the day I own another one
> - I screw up a lot...which is an understatement
> - I love to read
> - My MBTI is an ENFP
> - I own my own business
> - I drink a lot of coffee

- I just started putting my health as one of my top priorities – I want to do a triathlon in 2017
- I'm beautifully broken
- What some people call friends, I call family – and they are some of the most important people to me
- My kids teach me things every day
- I hate school, but I love learning
- My son is the mini version of me which excites and frightens the crap out of me
- My daughter gets away with murder because she's so cute
- My wife is a police officer – yes I'm a police "wife"
- My wife and I may be the only 30-somethings to own burial plots
- I enjoy beer and whiskey
- I listen to most types of music
- I used to play in bands...and still play bass from time to time
- I love to be near water and in God's creation
- I have three younger sisters
- I am called Uncle Jay by 13 kiddos – 2 of which are blood-related

Then I hit post. I switched the tab to Facebook and posted it on my newly minted page. I closed the computer and started sweating. Writing even that little bit felt free, and I knew the hard-internal work was just about to begin. I was excited. I was terrified. A couple of hours later, I peeked at Facebook. *Holy cow,* I thought, *People are reading and commenting on this.* It felt liberating to know I was being supported, and it scared me even more. Is this a space I can really be vulnerable? Is this a place I can really post my thoughts free from judgment? Does it really matter what others think or do here? *After all,* I thought, *I guess this is my page...*

CHAPTER 4

Finding a Therapist

OCTOBER 2016

When is the appropriate time to start talking about having another baby? *Is there ever one?* I wondered. My mind was swirling. I wanted to have another baby in our house, but I didn't know if I could go through the emotions of another pregnancy. *Was it genetic? Is that what happened to Ezra? Would we be putting ourselves through this all over again if we decided to have another?* Gina had just asked me one of those questions that swirl around your mind over and over. She walked into the kitchen, poured us coffees, sat beside me, and said, "I just...I just really want to hold another baby of ours."

"Me too," I said, "but...what if it happens again? What if we have to go through all of this again? I'm not sure if I can handle that."

"I know, it's always a risk...but all the doctors and nurses, they've said it's a freak thing; it could have happened to anyone."

"What about adoption?" I mentioned, "We could always foster or adopt or something like that. I just feel like I have so much more love to give."

"Yeah, adoption would be one option moving forward, I guess," Gina replied, "but at the same time, it's only been a month, so let's just keep talking about the options."

It was only a month and a half since Ezra had been delivered, and we were talking about having another baby, putting ourselves in the position to potentially be broken again. I had started going down a pretty heavy Google black hole looking up grief. I was looking up things like the stages of grief, how I was supposed to be feeling, and whether there was an end date to this thing called grief. I wanted to make sure I was as informed as possible so that I could best help the people around me.

In order to keep our commitments to each other, we established a nightly routine. We would sit down and ask each other two questions. The first was, "How was your day?" The second was a little more hard-hitting: "How was your heart today?" This started the same day we sat down and made our commitments to each other a little over a month ago.

So that evening, when we sat down after getting the kids to bed, Gina asked me the routine question: "So, how's your heart today, JD?"

"Well, today it's doing pretty good...I feel like I'm handling all of this pretty well lately, but there's still so much pain around it, so I'm trying to enter back into that pain slowly, bit by bit. You know?" She nodded.

"Sometimes I wonder," Gina said, "if we're really doing this right. This whole grieving thing, are we really doing this in a way that's genuinely helpful?"

This is where Gina and I are very different, I thought. She's so process driven, which is probably why she does so well at her job. I couldn't imagine doing her job. Ever since I knew Gina, she wanted to be a police officer. When she finished high school, she went on to police college, started volunteering, and got herself a part-time job as she worked towards her goal. After college, she started applying to police stations.

She wouldn't take no for an answer, and before long, she was up at Ontario Police College before she was even 21 I couldn't imagine doing her job, seeing what she has seen, or doing what she has done. She serves a population many of us haven't seen or spent too much time with. She doesn't typically get a lot of accolades from the general public either for the type of job she has.

I have always been envious of some of the training that she gets to do. Things like defensive tactics training, or where they go in and clear out a building looking for the shooter, or the driver's training, where they practice coming in and out of skids. Some of it seems pretty cool, but I wouldn't survive as a police officer.

The overarching culture is a little different as well. Many folks in the profession have seen some pretty terrible things, but how many are getting the help they need to process what they've seen? In many ways, it's similar to most male-dominated, patriarchal systems that would rather drain their sorrows in alcohol, make crude comments, and pretend everything is okay. Yes, it's a culture that is changing due to some amazingly strong and courageous people, and change takes a lot of time.

"Sometimes I wonder," Gina said, "if we're doing this right. This whole grieving thing, are we really doing this in a way that's genuinely helpful?"

She paused for a moment. "Maybe we should go to counseling…you know, just to make sure we're doing this whole grieving thing right."

I never thought I would hear those words come from her mouth, given her experiences in the police force, and it was nice to know that we were on the same page. I always tell people, "Maybe you should go to a professional and talk with them about what's going on in your life." I come from a philosophy that everyone should be in counseling, but I had never actually been. "You're right," I said, "I don't know that we need to go to see if we're actually grieving right, but I think it's a good idea for us to go and talk to someone."

Gina reminded me that we have a service through our church that provides counseling with some great counselors, so she promised to call and get more information about who we might be able to talk with. I had only three conditions: 1) they had to be a licensed counselor; 2) they had to have experience in trauma and grief, and; 3) they had to be doing this for a while – in other words, I wanted the counselor that the counselors went to when they needed help.

For most of my career, I've been a mediator and coach, helping people in conflict situations. I get to sit with them, ask them questions, hear their stories, and find out what's going on for them. So, there are a lot of similarities between coaching/mediation and counseling. Many of my clients would call me a counselor, mainly because that is the closest thing they know.

Counselors and conflict management professionals can sometimes ask similar questions to get to the root issues, and they often use similar strategies to help people get comfortable sharing their stories—techniques like silence, reframing, and paraphrasing (to name a few). If I was going to do counselling, I wanted the person that counsellors went to for therapy. Not because I didn't think someone without significant experience wouldn't know what they were talking about, but I wasn't looking for someone that I could talk "shop" with. I wanted someone to see through my bullshit and ask me the tough questions. I wanted someone to see through me and help me to do the same. I also wanted someone who had done their own work, someone who wasn't just talking the talk but had done the personal work so that they were healthy individuals. So, I told Gina, "Look for someone that counsels the counsellors."

Shortly after that call, I got a message from Gina: "Hey...so they gave me four people that meet our criteria." There was only one more problem with finding a counselor I hadn't anticipated.

Before I started working in the conflict and leadership transformation field with organizations and churches, I was a family mediator. I was the guy you called when your marriage was no longer a viable option, and you needed a process that would keep the needs of the children front and centre so that you and your partner could amicably separate your belongings and plan for the future with your newly organized family. During that time, some of my referrals would come from counsellors who provided couples guidance on improving their relationship. Unfortunately, for many reasons, some people did not thrive in that type of counselling relationship, and their marriage broke down after exhausting that option to attempt to save it. So, family therapists would sometimes recommend me to their clients who were pursuing this marriage exit, and as a result, I knew a fair number of counselors.

Gina gave me the names of the four potential people so I could do my initial Google search. Looking over the list of names, I realized I knew all but one. The other three were all steady referral sources in my mediation practice.

"Well," I said to Gina, "looks like we have one option, so let's set up a meeting with her to see if she'll be helpful."

So, we set up our first counselling session.

On the day of, we were a little nervous. *What are we going to talk about? Should we talk about what we're going to talk about before we get there? How much do we let her know? How much of our souls do we bare?* As we walked up to the building, I jokingly said to Gina, "Oh, by the way, I have a few surprises for us to talk about today...." Gina glared at me. "You better not," she replied.

"Joke, joke," I said as Gina let go of my hand and punched me in the arm. "We're going to discuss these violent outrages, though."

We entered the office and said "hello" as we were led to the couch. As we got settled in our spots, Gina spoke up. "So, where do we start?"

"Anywhere you want," the counsellor said.

Gina started to sniffle and then cry. "Okay, I guess I'll start at the beginning of why we're here," she said, launching into our story. For most of that conversation, I sat there. It's not that I had nothing to say; it just felt that Gina needed to release what was on her mind. It felt like she had things that needed to escape outside her, and I realized this was the first time she had told her son's story.

I had told the story multiple times already; sometimes, I was there, present in my body as I told it, feeling each painful memory being recalled, the warmness of tears on my cheeks, the subtle gasping for air, the life being taken out of me. Other times, I left my body, compartmentalized, and let my voice and head tell the story while I emotionally checked out. But for Gina, this was her first time, and she felt every emotion as if it was just happening.

So, I sat there, being supportive, that presence that helped hold her up. She cast looks between the ground, the counsellor, and me. I sat there, sending her every warm and loving thought I could possibly give so she could speak, feel, and experience the uninterrupted silence that occasionally permeated the air.

As she talked, I couldn't help noticing the strategies and tactics that the counsellor used. I couldn't help it; my work and training had become such a big part of my life that I took it around everywhere I went. When you own your own business, you learn quickly that it's really difficult to "turn it off." To turn off conversations as mere business opportunities, to see experiences as learnings that could be shared later, to turn off your brain and really be present without a looming to-do list that needed to be done. My work, training, and experiences in conflict and leadership had become something I believe in with such ferocity that I couldn't help but incorporate all of it into my life. Did that mean I was always saying the right thing or listening when I shouldn't be speaking? Not at all, but I had trained my "inner observer" to recognize when I wasn't operating out of a place of my best self.

Noticing these things made me realize that this was not the counsellor for me, that she would not be the one to see through the bullshit I told myself or provide the right questions to help me sort through my own experiences. It was through no fault of the counsellor, but we weren't a good fit. But for Gina? I could tell Gina felt comfortable with her. So at that moment, I knew that this was not the place to do my grief and personal work; this was the place to be supportive and loving so that Gina could build trust with the counsellor and no longer need me present.

That night, Gina asked me the question we had been asking each other each night, "How's your heart today?" We talked about our experiences with the counsellor. We decided that, although this was not the counsellor for me, I would continue to come along for the next little while until Gina felt comfortable going on her own. We also agreed that I would still come every few months with Gina so that we could both do a check-in with the counsellor so that I could be there to support Gina, and so that Gina could support me in my journey as well. "In the meantime, JD, it looks like you'll have to find someone for you."

The following week I found myself sitting on my back deck with Russ, one of my best friends. There's something you need to know about Russ. He is a man's man. He's a diesel mechanic and can virtually fix anything that is broken. If you ever visit him, you'll rarely find him in the house because he's in the garage trying to figure something out. When you walk into that garage to visit, one of the first things he'll do is hand you a beer. We've been good friends for eighteen years already, and we've been through a lot, though nothing like this.

A couple of days before Ezra was delivered, Russ left for his two-week shift up in northern Canada. Then, on the night of our devastating blessing, he called me.

"Hey Jay...ummm...I'm really sorry about all of this, and I wish there was something I could do...I'm trying to get out of this hell hole, but they're being massive assholes about leaving."

He was trying to get the company to give him his security clearance so he could come home early and visit us, but they would let him go home only two days before he was normally scheduled to leave. So, he was stuck there. Russ, being the friend that he is, did the next best thing: he called me every other evening to check in on how we were doing. I would sit there on the phone and give him a report on how everyone was going. Then I'd promptly hang up the phone and break down.

I couldn't just hang up the phone with him sitting in front of me, though. He checked in as we sat there, drinking a beer on the deck. "So, how's it going, Jason?"

"It's going, man," I replied, "Gina's still having a rough time with everything. The kids, Carson especially, will break into tears without any notice, and if I'm being honest, I'm pretty wrecked myself."

Russ just sat there, looking at me, nodding his head up and down slowly, thinking to himself, but he didn't say anything. The look on his face simply said, "Go on..."

"I know...it's only been a month," I said, "but it feels like I should be further along. But, at the same time, I don't know what that would even look like either. I know they say time heals all, but I'm starting to think that's just bullshit. I mean, does it really ever get better, or do we simply become more comfortable with the pain and grief? Like, it never really leaves us, but we just become more comfortable with it, so it feels like it doesn't hurt as bad."

"Maybe," Russ said, "I don't know, man. I can only imagine what you guys are going through."

"Man, I wouldn't wish this on my worst enemy. Yet, at the same time, I feel like swearing at God. You know? I know through all of this, God will be here supporting me, holding me up when I can't do it myself, and I know that something will come out of this. Like, I'm going to learn something about myself, about my community, about God himself, but....fuck. Was this the way to do it? Wasn't there another way?"

The moment I said that, I knew there was no other way. I knew that's the way God and I had worked with each other in the past. I'm a little dense and stubborn when it comes to listening to God. Kind of as if God will send me a lot of little messages, some I'll notice, some I'll see in hindsight, and some that I'm sure I have never picked up on. When I feel a nudging in a certain direction, I start to build my case of why I can't. I'm always reminded of Moses. He walks up to this burning bush, and stands there dumbfounded as he listens to God tell him what God has planned before he squeaks out, "You want to send me? You want to send me? What do I even tell them when they ask who sent me?" Then God lays out his great plan to persuasively convince Pharaoh to let his people go, and what does Moses do again?

I just picture Moses looking down at the ground, kicking some dirt around, and saying, "Uhhh...but what if they don't believe me that you sent me?" God stands there shaking his head, "Well Moses, just throw down your staff on the ground, or put your hand in your cloak...go ahead, give it a try!"

You would think that Moses would reflect, "Holy cow! I just saw my walking stick turn into a freaking snake! And I just had leprosy for thirty seconds! Dang! This is a powerful God!" But no, that's not what he thought. At least, that's not what he said. Moses instead says to this powerful God, "Uh God.... uh...sorry...I should call you 'I am'... uh....yeah, I don't really have a way with words, so I think you should really pick someone else. I mean, there are others out there that would be way better for the job, don't you think?

Yeah, I do something similar. When I look back on my life, I can see the times that I had similar conversations, well, not freeing my people from slavery and into the promised land types of conversation, but definitely conversations when God said to me, "Jason, go and do this." And I certainly responded with, "Well...you really think that's a good idea? Hmmm, let's sleep on it..."

I can think of countless times when God said to me, "Hey Jason, sooooo... remember that time you were going to sleep on this? Yeah, it's almost time to get moving." To which I usually responded, "So, God, you just used the word almost, that means not yet—right? Okay, I'm just going back to sleep for a little longer."

Then BAM! I get hit with a figurative 2x4 to the side of the head, and I hear the voice - "Jason, get moving! It's time!" And then I go. I take the job that God led me to; I send that message to the friend I should have sent long ago. That's when I start making changes in my life and I start acting on something I probably should have done years ago.

"You know what, Russ —" I snapped back into where I was — "If this happened to me two years ago, I would have been a much bigger wreck than you can imagine."

"What do you mean?" Russ asked.

"I can see all the places where God has been preparing me for this. Just over two years ago, I was having some definite struggles, and God put some much-needed conversations in place to smack me around a little. Then I started my Master's in Leadership, where they literally broke me down into little pieces. I mean, I completely took myself apart, piece by piece, and had to look at my life, and I didn't really like what I saw. I mean, life was good, but I could see the areas where I needed to grow, the areas that I was avoiding because it made life easier; I could see where I was running away. So, through that process those two years, I've been challenged by stuff that has slowly put me back together in a way that leads me to be a completely different person than I was two years ago. I mean, I don't think God is doing this to me on purpose, but I do think that he's spent some serious time preparing me for this."

Russ just sat there and nodded, taking it all in. I knew he was a bit uncomfortable. This wasn't our usual conversation. We would talk about real stuff, we would talk about some of the problems in our lives, some of the challenges, but neither of us knew what to do with this. I mean, how do you, as a man, start talking about what's going on deep inside of you? Do you tell it all? Do you even know what you're actually feeling? Is that what a man really does?

Most of the men in my life rarely talked about their emotions. I can count on one hand how many men I have seen cry. My impression of men growing up was that if you had any emotion other than anger, you should be stuffing that shit way down. And if you were successful in stuffing all those unwelcome feelings way down, one day, it would get so bottled up that it would explode into fists. The men in my life typically wouldn't shed a tear or even show much emotion, and they especially didn't have deep conversations about emotion, did they?

I'll never forget being in my early twenties and sending my mom a text: *Put today in the history books;, I officially became a man today.* My mom, being the worrier that she is, replied, *Jason...I'm a little nervous as to what this means...*

That was the day I received my first toolbox. In many ways, it was a rite of passage of what it meant to be a man. Maybe it's because it's taken me thirty-some-odd years to grow a beard. Or that I grew up in a house full of women (three sisters!). Or even that I'm not someone who does well working with tools. Often the words "man" and "Jason" typically haven't been used in the same sentence — unless it started with "Aww man...why'd you do that, Jason?"

Actually, tools are probably a good metaphor for men. Tools fix things, are tough, and have a specific purpose or function. But, of course, the same could be said about some men.

Historically (at least for the last 100 years), the main purpose for men has been to put food on the table by going to a job that took them away from the house for at least 8 to 10 hours a day.

Unfortunately, we see men that are still trying to keep that purpose. Look at the difference in wages between men and women and tell me I'm wrong. When I got married, I used to joke with friends that the only reason I got married when I did was because I was graduating from university with a fair amount of debt, and my wife already had a job making good money. Even as ideal as this was, it sure didn't do anything for my alleged "man-card." For the first couple of years of marriage, I was constantly second-guessing my role in our relationship — after all; I had always been told that it was the man's job to make the money of the house. The money that paid the mortgage, the bills, that put food on the table. It would take years to build my business to get close to my wife's income.

After building my business to where my income was close to my wife's, I started a new business with three incredible humans and took a huge pay cut. This time, though, I didn't think twice about my role as a provider. I have many roles within my marriage, roles that I now recognize are just as import- ant: feeding and caring for kids (including changing dirty diapers), vacuum- ing, preparing meals, cleaning the house, doing groceries, and so much more. Roles that have too often been affiliated with "women's work." Newsflash, guys, it's our role too.

Men are tough. Most of the guys I know are really tough. They look tough, and they would throw fists if anyone crossed them. They're tough. Our culture today says that men must be tough, especially when it comes to anything remotely emotional. For example, the strength of a man in sorrow is shown in his tearless face. Tears are a sign of weakness for men. If you get hurt, you don't cry - Fuck no, you just swear a lot. Men are so tough they won't even ask for help.

Years ago, my brother-in-law, Will, got in a nasty accident at his summer job. He was working with a buddy of his painting houses to earn some money and put it towards his career goals. One day that summer, he was precariously on a ladder leaning up against a house painting a window sill when he slipped off the ladder and came crashing down on, of all things, a giant gargoyle. He punctured his pancreas badly. So badly that the doctors said that his wounds were similar to a gunshot wound and that he was lucky to be alive.

That accident would lead to weeks of hospitalization followed by weeks of recovery at home on the couch. We often visited to chat with Will, helping him pass the hours as he lay on the couch, trying not to move. It was taxing on the whole family, but we joined together to offer care and support for him as he journeyed toward health.

I was in the middle of it, supporting my wife and mother-in-law, especially as they wrestled with the whole situation. I can't remember shedding a tear the whole time because that's not what I was there to do. They needed a rock; they needed someone who would be there so that they could express their emotions, their frustrations, and their worst-case scenario planning so that we could anticipate the worst-possible outcome and be prepared. I was there for the late nights, and emergency phone calls, trying to be the one that would support them when they didn't know where else to turn.

A couple of weeks later, I found myself alone in church. I walked through the sanctuary, my mind turning over the events that had happened in the weeks past and sat down at the piano. Before I knew what was happening, I started playing an old song I wrote that I never put any lyrics to, singing from the bottom of my heart. It didn't take long for the tears to start flowing from my eyes, staining my cheeks. I sat there for an hour, singing, and crying; feeling all those feelings that I was desperately trying to run from.

Men don't need help; we're tough. But why do we celebrate this stoic tearlessness? Why do we insist on maintaining our outward toughness when we're bleeding inwardly? Why must we mask our suffering and troubles to maintain our external shell of toughness?

In the last two months since Ezra was delivered, I've had the honour and privilege to see men who were so tough they embraced their own vulnerability. They welcomed their pain. They embraced their tears. A couple of weeks ago, I was sitting in a coffee shop reading a book about grief with tears streaming down my face. That's tough. As men, we too often take this journey of internal bleeding alone; we seemingly pride ourselves on not needing anybody.

"We're tough; we got this...we don't need anybody to get us through this." That's not tough. That's being a coward. I know; I've been there. We think it's being the tough person at the time, but really, it's being a coward. It's guarding ourselves so that nobody gets a glimpse of the real us. It's guarding ourselves so that nobody sees how we really feel about what's happening right before us.

Tough is knowing you can't do this alone. Tough is reaching out and calling a friend to help you through it. Tough is leaning on your community when you can barely stand up by yourself. Tough is entering into vulnerability and baring your inner bleeding so that pressure can be applied to the wound instead of us bleeding out on the sidewalk because we were too proud to accept help.

Men also do this thing where they fix things. My best friends are ridiculously handy. They can literally fix anything with their hands. Recently I told Russ that I would send Carson to live with them for summers because I had literally taught Carson everything I knew about fixing stuff. For as long as I can remember, I've always been told that men are supposed to be fixers. You bring them a problem, and they fix it. This works great—until it doesn't. Not everything can be fixed, and too often, men are the ones who are trying to fix a problem that is beyond repair.

And when men can't fix the problem, or they don't perceive it as a problem, we simply say something like, *just walk it off, leave it in the past and move forward with your life.*

Not all problems are meant to be solved, though. A friend once told me, "Is this a problem to solve or a tension to navigate?" And that's exactly the question. Not all problems are meant to be solved. Problems can be solved, and conflicts can be resolved, but others, like polarities or tensions, can only be navigated. Some things go deeper, right to our core, and those are the ones that we simply have to journey alongside. Those are the ones that never go away. Those are the ones that are unsolvable.

When Ezra was delivered, I desperately wanted to fix the situation, but I couldn't. My friends, both men and women, wanted to fix the situation or even alleviate the pain a little. But they couldn't. That's where you can tell who is a real man and who isn't. The real men are the ones that will step into uncertainty and not try and fix the situation. The real men will simply sit there, ask you some questions, and listen without judgement. The real men are there to help when they are asked because they know how difficult it is to even ask for help. It's hard to pick up the phone, call a friend and say, "I need your help; we need to talk." Talking is the kryptonite for too many men. Men get so caught up in the physical acts of helping that it's too often forgotten that there's a real live human being beneath each man's exterior that must be attended to.

All my life, I've wanted to grow up to be a man, and all my life, I've felt like I've never measured up I was too emotional; I couldn't use my hands to fix things; I arranged my whole work schedule around Gina's work schedule so that I could watch the kids while she was at work. *And no, it's not called babysitting in case you're asking; it's called parenting.* Men seemed to have it all: they can fix things, they are tough, nothing phases them, and they fulfill an essential role.

For the last thirty-some-odd years, I wanted to be like those men because that's what I was told was manly. But that's not a man. Yes, men can fix things, be tough, and have a specific purpose. And they are also emotional, supportive, and loyal. I think wedding proposals are probably when men are genuinely the manliest.

This is one time in a man's life that he truly becomes vulnerable for his partner. In my circles, the man starts by approaching the parents of his girlfriend, especially her father. "Can...ahem...can I have your blessing on asking your daughter to marry me?" It's a nerve-wracking question, and it's an awkward conversation, but it's important because it's essential for a man to be willing to approach another and have a vulnerable conversation. A conversation that says, "Hey, I really love your daughter, like I'm really head-over-heels about her, so much so that I want to spend the rest of my life with her."

I was beyond nervous when I went to ask Gina's parents for their blessing. I borrowed my friend's car and tried convincing him to come with me as a buffer. He said no. Apparently, it was something I had to do on my own.

Then, after that blessing is obtained, men have to plan out how they are actually going to ask this woman to spend the rest of their lives with them. That's kind of a big deal!

I remember when I asked Gina to marry me. Nothing went right that night. We were going to go to this great place that neither of us had been to before, a place that had a lake and a beach. Both of those things Gina and I love! I checked the weather that morning and quickly realized things would not work out in my favour as it was supposed to rain that evening. And not just a little, but a lot! I held out hope that the rain wasn't going to interfere with my plans, but sooner or later I had to face the facts: the rain was going to be a problem. So we went to one of the restaurants close to Gina's house that we liked—Turtle Jacks. Not a special place for most people, but for us, we had been there many times. We grabbed a spot so that we could have some supper. I had my usual three-cheese Cajun chicken penne. I typically don't do well with spice, it never sits right in my stomach, and my nerves were already putting my stomach in knots. Typically, the penne is pretty calm on the spices, but not that night. They must have added some extra spice to mine, so I was sweating, and my stomach was already overly jumpy. My mind was racing: *Should I do it now? What about now? But there are too many people around! We can't do this in the middle of a restaurant!* After supper, we walked back to her car. The heavy rain had stopped, and it was just spitting finally. I opened her side of the door, and as she was talking about grabbing a coffee for the way home, I kneeled down on one knee. "Gina..." I said, trying to draw her attention, "You mean the world to me, and I want to spend the rest of my life exploring this world with each other. Will you marry me?"

Her tears started flowing. Taking those tears as a definite yes, I slipped the ring on her finger, kissed her, and jumped in the driver's seat.

I think wedding proposals are when men are truly being a man. This is one of the times in a man's life that he truly becomes vulnerable for his partner. He gets down on one knee, takes his partner's hand, and softly whispers, "Will you marry me?" He doesn't get upset when his partner starts to cry; heck, maybe he even has one or two tears rolling down his own cheek. But at that moment, he's truly a man. He makes himself vulnerable. He's there for his partner without distraction, he's truly expressing his love.

We need to propose more often.

CHAPTER 5

His Name is Evan

NOVEMBER 2016

As the months progressed, Gina and I continued exploring the possibility of having another baby. At the beginning of November, we stepped into the doctor's office, the one that had delivered Ezra, so that we could have some follow-up conversation around what had happened with our son. We stepped out of the waiting room into the doctor's office, and eyes pierced through me with equal parts concern and empathy. "How are the two of you doing?" she asked.

Gina started to cry and said, "We're doing." She wiped off her tears. "We just had a couple of questions for you."

"Yeah," I said, "a couple of questions we're hoping you might be able to speak to. We definitely don't expect you to be able to answer them all, but any information you might have or thoughts you might have would be helpful." I sat up a little straighter.

"Sure," the doctor said, "I'll do my best to answer anything you're wondering about."

Gina breathed, "You'd mentioned on the phone that you'd gotten the test results back from the placenta that was looked at through the hospital. We're just wondering if any additional information came out of that?"

"Well," the doctor took a long breath, "nothing conclusive came out of it. However, there are a few theories." She took another long breath. "One that some of the nurses had suggested was that Ezra had an aneurism, another is that the cord got wrapped around his neck, which we're pretty sure isn't the case, and the last theory is that the umbilical cord wasn't perfectly centred in the middle of the placenta. So, when labour started, it cut off the blood flow passing through the cord." She looked at us both.

"But they're all just theories. Without doing the autopsy, we couldn't look any further into it, and to be honest; I'm not sure an autopsy would have helped. Are you both struggling with why this all happened?"

"No," Gina said, "we've accepted it, and we both know that there's nothing that we could have done to stop it. I mean, all the ultrasounds were perfectly good; there was never any sign that the baby was in trouble or at risk of anything, so no, we're not struggling with that anymore; just curious, that's all. It's just, it's just—one of those fluke things."

"I know that doesn't make it easier," the doctor said, "but that's exactly it; it's a fluke thing, a really crappy fluke thing, but I've poured over every ultrasound and test from your pregnancy, and we haven't found anything conclusive."

"Thank you for doing that," I said, "it really a lot to us. So... the other thing that kind of rattles around my brain is – is there a chance that this was genetic? I mean, yes, we've had two other fully healthy and active kids, but could it be something within our genetics that make this all happen? I... I'm just wondering if we were to try and have another child...what are the chances of this happening again?" Gina nodded her head.

"We've been talking about having another child," Gina said as tears started to roll down her face again, "but Jason's a little concerned that this could happen again."

"The odds of it happening again are the same as with Ezra," the doctor began. "It's definitely not a genetic thing; I can say that with confidence. Looking over all the tests, ultrasounds, and placenta, it doesn't seem to be a genetic thing, so the chances of it happening again are the same as when you became pregnant with Ezra. However,..."

Oh crap, I thought, *here it comes. The, however, ... However, I would advise against having another child, or however, you now have an increased risk of having a miscarriage, or...*

"However, you would be considered as having a high-risk pregnancy, Gina, if you were to decide to have another child. Which, actually, in your circumstances, might be beneficial."

We both looked at her, a little confused. "Would you want to have midwife care again?" the doctor asked.

"Yes, of course," Gina said, "We loved our midwives, and they've been so supportive of us through all of this...through the pregnancy, the delivery, after Ezra was born. They've been wonderful."

"I agree," said the doctor, "you had two excellent midwives. What I mean is that because you've lost a baby, you would be considered high risk, which means we would be monitoring you more and you would be able to have midwives, and an OBGYN."

"So...we could request that we have you again...you know...if we decide to have another kid?" Gina asked.

"You sure could." A smile crept over the doctor's face. "It would be your choice, of course, but you could request me, and if you did, I would be more than honoured to walk with you through pregnancy, especially if you had the same midwives! I love working with them, and we have a great relationship, so I would be honoured to be a part of that team."

"Okay," Gina said, "that's really good to know. Thank you."

We walked out of the doctor's office, both a little teary-eyed..."So what do you think, Jay?" Gina asked.

"Oh jeez, Gina, you know what, we've been talking a lot about this, and you know my biggest concern has been that it was something genetic. So that's why I was pushing adoption so hard; it just seems easier. Yeah, I know, it's probably a bit of a waitlist, and there are some other risks or possibilities with going that route, but it just feels so much easier."

"I know, Jay, I just...I just don't think I'm done with having babies of our own yet, and our table somehow feels not quite full. I know that we'll never replace Ezra, and I'm not trying to do that; I just know that I want to have another of our own. Our own blood."

"You know what, babe," I said, "coming into this meeting with the doctor, I wasn't convinced we should give it a shot. But after hearing what she had to say, I said let's do it. I'm on board, 100%."

We agreed to sleep on it for a couple of weeks, neither of us wanting to feel like we were replacing Ezra, and we wanted to ensure we were both ready. However, I knew that it would be a rough nine months if we decided to have another one. Anxieties would be high, and what if we had the same outcome as we did with Ezra? I wasn't sure my heart could take going through this again.

I had experienced a part of love I had never experienced before. Yes, I had lost loved ones, but that was very different from losing a child. It was weird, actually, I didn't really think that Ezra would have this much impact on me. It made sense that it would on Gina — I mean, she carried the little guy around with her for the better part of a year. But for me? I didn't have the chance to get to know him.

I'm not much of a baby guy as it is. I have a rule; if the baby can't lift up or support its head, I don't want to hold it. All of our friends had had babies; I never held any of the children until they were a few months old. One of the first babies that I ever held, and that broke my hard-fast rule, was our first son Carson. I still remember the day Carson was born. I was so excited, so happy; my heart was bursting out of my chest. I couldn't wait to show him to the whole world! I didn't even think about my rule as I took him into my arms and stared deeply into his eyes.

But it was kind of weird for me to think that Ezra had such an impact on me since I didn't really know him. He never got a chance to smile at me or for me to show him how to take a slap shot. I never got the chance to feed him or tuck him into bed. And yet, I loved this child fiercely. I never had the chance to show him the world, but he was showing me the world through a whole new set of eyes. He was redefining love for me. He was making me see love through a whole new lens.

I never really thought about love this much either, other than how much God loves us. About eight years ago, I got a large tattoo on my right forearm that says, "Astonishing Love." When I got it, I actually wanted it to say "amazing love," but the word amazing had been thrown around so much that it had lost its meaning. So, I went with astonishing. The tattoo had a religious meaning for me. To me, it meant that we have all done some pretty stupid shit in our lives. Stolen things, done things to people we weren't proud of, lied through our teeth to avoid trouble, cheated on tests, and said things to people that were really mean. And yet, there was this God who said, "You are my child with whom I am well pleased." This powerful being who looked down on us and said, "You are my beloved"—all the while we're doing really dumb things!

To me, it was simply amazing.

To me, it was astonishing.

So, I got it tattooed on my arm so I could see it daily as a reminder. "You are loved, Jason Dykstra; you are beloved, God's child."

Over the years, though, that meaning took on new exploration. Our organization sat down about six years ago and defined our core values. The values that summed up our essence. How we behaved with each other and our clients, the values we felt were so important that they had to be part of our DNA. We came up with three words. Love. Listen. Lead.

Love people for who they are in that moment. Love them unconditionally, or from a more secular stance, show people unconditional positive regard. We are all made in God's image; we are all God's beloved, his children. We are all, as human beings, worthy of love and belonging.

Listen to the wisdom in every person, listen for the wisdom of the organization or community we are working in, and listen for God's leading in all situations and scenarios.

And lastly, lead. Lead with a sense of courage, integrity, and honour. Say the things that need to be said, take people to difficult places so that we can lie in the muck and wrestle with varying perspectives. Lead from a place of wholeheartedness.

Those values took on a life of their own in our organization. Every discussion from that point on was steeped in those values. It wasn't uncommon for someone to ask, "So how are you loving these people?" or "What is that scenario trying to teach them or us?" We placed those values at our core, and miraculously, big decisions were made easier because we viewed all things through the lens of our values. How we treated each other was viewed through the lens of those values. How we treat those around us is viewed through those values.

Those values also took on a life of their own in my personal life. I started to let those values deep into my insides, and before I knew it, it was also how I viewed the world—especially this value of love. I started to think about it all the time: what did it mean to love? How do we best show love to others?

Three years ago, we moved from the decently-small city of Cambridge, which has roughly 150,000 people, to a little village just south of Cambridge called St. George. St. George is quaint. We have one stoplight, but all the necessities. A grocery store, two bars, a coffee shop, a flower shop, a hardware store, three pizza places, and even a second-hand shop. And of course, at the village centre, the elementary school and the hockey arena. Our village boasts a population of around 3,000 people.

The moment that we moved in, it felt like home. Gina and I came from smaller towns, so it was a great match for our personalities. We decided to be intentional about our move, so we put our son in the public school in town instead of the Christian school as our childhood had been like. We don't have anything against the Christian school — in fact; we support it: however, we wanted to be intentional with where we were living. We wanted to get to know our neighbours and the folks in town. We wanted to show them love.

About a year after moving into town, we heard of a precious little boy who went to our son's school. He was only a couple of years ahead of Carson. He was a ordinary boy, and he did ordinary boy stuff. There wasn't anything particularly amazing about this little boy. He liked Sponge Bob Squarepants and superheroes, and he loved Christmas.

His name was Evan. But there was something remarkable about this little boy. He brought an entire town together. You see, Evan had an inoperable brain tumour, and he was falling victim to it at a rapid pace. Around September, the doctors told Evan's mom that she should think about celebrating Christmas early for Evan because they didn't think would make it to see Christmas Day. So, in mid-October, Evan's mom planned to go out for a special Christmas supper with her little boy. Evan's family approached a couple of businesses on the main strip and asked them to put up some Christmas lights so that when they were on their way home from dinner, Evan could see some Christmas cheer.

One of the business owners posted the letter to Facebook and encouraged the town to share it and put up their Christmas lights early so that Evan could tour the town for his last Christmas. She asked a town to bring Christmas to a little boy that needed our support. Our love. So, people put up their lights.

It would have been an incredible story if it ended there. A little boy in search of one more Christmas with his family, and a town so touched by this child that they brought Christmas to him in October. But it didn't stop there. There was talk of a parade. A Christmas parade throughout our town. Our little town of 3,000 people. The applications started to pour in more than anyone expected. There were hundreds of applications of businesses and individuals who wanted to participate in Evan's parade, hundreds of people who wanted to show their support for the family, and hundreds of people who wanted to give this little, amazing boy their love.

The day came, in late October, for the night of the parade. Our family and our friends gathered our kids and walked over to the block near Evan's house.

There were people littered throughout the streets. It was supposed to rain that night, but God must have decided this was a time to celebrate, not to shed tears of grief, so God held back the rain. To this day, it was the best parade our little town had ever experienced. Sponge Bob Squarepants and the minions were walking in the parade, fire trucks and police motorcycles cruised through the town, and floats upon floats passed us by. Then came the main event: Santa and his sleigh being pulled by the reindeer. As Santa reached Evan's house, he stopped, and there was Evan. Evan joined Santa on his sleigh with the biggest smile I have ever seen. Pure love.

It was the saddest, most beautiful sight that I have encountered. Sad in that this little boy was dying. Sad in that his mom and family were losing their beloved child. And yet, there was a whole community, and more, drawn together by this wonderful, spectacular, and overly ordinary boy because of his love. His love for Christmas brought together a whole community of people to share in that love. In total, more than 7,000 people packed into the streets of our little town. More than double the population.

That day, it wasn't the end of October. It was Christmas.

There wasn't anything particularly incredible about Evan; his family are average people, he hadn't done anything extraordinary, and he doesn't have any particular special skills or talents that I know of. He was a seven-year-old boy. But something about him brought out the best of an entire community.

I like to think of myself similarly. There's nothing particularly special about me. I'm a normal person. I have struggles just like everyone else, yet something happens when we challenge each other to lead from within. Something extraordinary happens when we live out of our values and out of love. 1 Corinthians says that love is patient and kind. It's not jealous, boastful, proud, or rude. It doesn't even demand its own way. It's not irritable, it doesn't keep records of wrong and doesn't rejoice in injustices. It does, however, rejoice whenever the truth rings out. Love doesn't give up, it never loses faith, it's always hopeful and is enduring through every circumstance. Love never fails.

Love never fails. It changes us. It's a funny thing, this love business. We often think of it as passive when it's quite active. The dictionary says that love is a noun. But it seems to be more of a verb to me. Love never fails; it changes us. Love requires work, courage, and vulnerability. It transforms us, invites us to change, live into the discomfort it brings, and rumble with it. Love never fails; it changes us.

This idea of love I have struggled with over the years. It's like we've been in a bare-knuckled brawl. It's like when Jacob meets God in the middle of the night and wrestles with him. All these years, I have been living in love, exploring its depths, and wrestling with God about what love is really like. I thought I had it figured out, this whole love thing. I thought I had it defined.

Then we had Ezra, and the wrestling match began again. I had to start wrestling with God again about this thing called love. I realized that I had experienced this type of love before but couldn't quite express it. That night, when it was Christmas in October, Evan showed me a piece of this love. I stood there in the crowds experiencing the most heart-wrenching and heart-warming thing in my life. I didn't realize that love could do that. I didn't comprehend that love could tear your heart out and stomp all over it, only to refine the heart further.

And here I was again. Experiencing my heart being ripped out, thrown onto the ground, and repeatedly stomped on. I sat there and watched as my heart took a beating. I saw the bruises that it was receiving, the blood that was oozing from it, and it getting stronger and stronger. I could see with each punch that love grew. I could see with each kick that it continued to grow. Ezra showed me that nothing is too great for love. Love is patient, and it is kind. It never demands its own way. It doesn't keep records of wrongs; it doesn't rejoice in injustices. Love never gives up, never loses faith, never loses sight of hope, and it can endure every situation. Love never fails.

It may hurt like hell, yet love never fails. It may leave you feeling battered and bruised, yet love never fails. It may throw you on the ground and kick dirt all over you, yet love never fails.

The next day I was at our executive team meeting. I sat through the meeting with only one question on my mind that I had to ask my amazingly brilliant and soul-searching colleagues: "Where do you turn to when you need help?"

I work in an interesting field where the majority of my peers are significantly older than me. I remember one of the first conflict management industry events that I attended when I was starting in the field almost ten years ago. It was a meet-and-greet type of setting, and I walked in with my nerves jumping from one place in my body to the next. Several people I had met on Twitter were going to the event, individuals who had been in the conflict business for a number of years already and whom I had learned significantly from only meeting them in an online setting.

So, I was very excited but incredibly nervous to meet these people I considered icons in the field. These were people who were doing something very different than everyone else because they were embracing this thing called "social media." And they were the only people I actually knew there. So, when I arrived, I looked through the event that was full of people, and all I could see was a sea of grey hair. From my quick perusal of the room, it looked as if everyone had at least twenty-five years on me. I saw one of my "friends" that I had met on Twitter and walked over to him. "Hey, Colm, it's great to finally meet you in person!" Colm introduced me to a few of his colleagues and thus began my adventures into the world of conflict transformation and mediation. It was through introductions from these talented individuals who I met that set me on a trajectory to building my own business.

I just shut up and listened when I was in these people's presence. I listened to their success stories, "war" stories, and the stories in which they failed or missed an opportunity. I watched as they interacted with others, I watched as they sought to better themselves and the people around them, I watched to see the types of questions they asked and how they held themselves.

Shortly after this event I went to a workshop that introduced me to Elizabeth, one of my company's co-founders. I remember sitting there watching how Liz spoke, how she asked questions, how she taught the information, and how she facilitated the conversations. She took this work to a whole new level compared to other courses I had been in. I couldn't put my finger on it then, but she brought something to her work that I hadn't seen in other conflict professionals. I now realize it was depth. She had a depth of knowledge and experience in the content she taught, but you could tell this information was more than just that to her. These skills of conflict transformation weren't just skills needing to be developed. They were a way of life. The work of conflict transformation wasn't just something you forced or invited others to join in on. It was a journey that you went on with that person. In order to lead someone else through it, you had to experience it for yourself.

It was Liz who introduced me to William O'Brien's quote, "The success of an intervention is dependent on the interior condition of the intervenor." It's a quote that spoke to me so deeply and that she lived so fiercely that it has transformed me. It was that quote, and Liz's guidance, over the past eight years that really encouraged me to reach deep inside myself and start to actually get to know the real me. Not the me I pretended to be but the me I was being called into. I've reworked this quote in multiple ways over the years to fit the context that I was in. Such as, "The success of an organization is dependent on the interior conditions of its leaders" or "The success of a family is dependent on the interior condition of its parents." Regardless of its iteration, it always spoke one truth: the work of one's interior condition is a journey. It's a continuous exercise that consistently needs to be tended to.

It seemed as if Elizabeth and Evan had something in common. They were regular, ordinary people that possessed incredible talent. They could show up, be who they were, and transform the people around them.

I started to see things in new ways; I started to see how some of my reactions to things were not very helpful. I came to realize that I needed to work on my listening skills. I have been an emotional person all my life, which I usually attribute to growing up in a family of women, but I know it's just my wiring. It's a part of me that I've always attempted to hide from others because that's not what I thought it was to be a man. The men I knew held back their tears when they were hurting because tears were a sign of weakness. I've realized, though, that the men I knew held back their emotions because they didn't know what to do with them. So, they just stuffed them down, as far down as they could, so they didn't have to face them. I thought that's what I was supposed to do too, so I hid from my emotions. I feared them.

However, if I was going to help others through the emotions of conflict, I needed to start paying attention to what I was doing with my own emotions. And thus, my life became one large experiment on the journey of self-awareness. I started reading self-help books and entering every conversation I could find that would explore what was going on for me inside. The deeper I went internally, the more I was able to be effective and helpful to my clients.

I would never have learned this, and so many other important lessons, if I hadn't surrounded myself with wise individuals who I now have the privilege to call colleagues and friends. So, when it came to asking where I could find help dealing with the grief that had taken over my life, I knew whom I had to turn to. As the meeting ended, I turned to my colleagues and said, "I feel like I've learned a lot about myself and many life lessons through the loss of Ezra, and I feel like more digging needs to be done there. Where did you turn when you've felt like this in your life?"

It took courage to ask the question, though it always takes courage to ask the important questions. The important questions always seem to put you in a place of vulnerability, a raw place where you must bear a portion of your heart and soul to someone. So, the question didn't quite roll off my tongue. I struggled to get it out.

Keith said, "When I find myself needing help like that, I usually 'treat' it like a spiritual problem. I've always felt like it's this inner spiritual battle that's happening inside of me, so I typically go to my spiritual director."

Mary replied, "Yeah, I'm a little different that way. I have a therapist that I see who happens to have a spiritual background, so I get a little bit of both."

Elizabeth chimed in as well. "I have a friend that I go see that does a mixture of massage and reading energies. I've always walked away from there with a deeper sense of the direction I need to be heading in."

"Hmmm... thanks so much for sharing with me," I said. "Would you mind sending me some people that you think I might click with that I could research a little?"

It wasn't long before I was in a dark Google tunnel, knee-deep in spiritual advisors, therapists, and alternate ways to explore and mine the lessons that I sought. While I was scrolling through a list of spiritual advisors, I came across a familiar name. It was the name of one of my old psychology professors with whom I had taken a couple of classes. *Hmmm... I thought, a therapist who also does spiritual direction...*

So, I gave her a call and set up an appointment.

A week later, I found myself sitting in her office, looking around. I was sitting on an older couch with two throw pillows on either side. I moved the pillows behind my back and put them on my lap. Beside me was a little end table with a pottery-made bowl with a candle inside it. Across from me was a low chair that the therapist, Bev, sat in. To my left was a big window that beamed rays of light into the office. There was a smell of incense or some sort of candle that had been burning before my arrival.

"So, Jason," Bev said, "where do you want to start? You mentioned on the phone that you weren't sure if you were looking for a therapist or a spiritual advisor. Either way, it's important for us both to ensure this is the right relationship for us. I want to make sure that you're comfortable with me and that I feel I can journey alongside you in your path. So where do you want to start?"

Good question, I thought; where the hell do I start?

"I know," Bev said, "let's start by taking a moment of silence so that we can really enter this room, this space, and whenever you feel like you're ready, you can start in the place you feel led to start with."

I nodded my head, sat straight up with my back against the couch, and placed my feet flat against the floor. I set each hand palm-down on my thigh, took a breath, and slowly closed my eyes. I could feel myself enter the room, all the emotions swooping in like a hurricane, and the tears start flowing down my cheeks.

"Well," I said, "I guess I should start with the biggest thing that's ever happened to me. My son."

I led her through the story, talked about some of my family dynamics, and felt heard for the first time in a long time. Finally, here was someone who would sit here and listen without judgment, with her full attention, to what was going on for me.

As the time came to a close, I said to Bev, "So, as you can see, a few things are going on in my life, and I feel like the biggest hurdle that I'm facing, or the biggest lessons for me in all of this, is a spiritual one, so I feel like I need some spiritual direction to take me deeper into the pain, the grief, and loss. But... but... I know that once we get down there, I will realize just how fucked up I am, so I might need some counseling as well."

She nodded slowly, "You've been through a lot in the past few months, Jason, and it would be an honour for me to walk with you through this journey."

CHAPTER 6

A Blue Christmas

DECEMBER 2016

Every holiday and birthday that had passed since Ezra's birth held a little piece of pain. We had already made it through two birthdays and Thanksgiving, but now Christmas was coming. Gina loves Christmas. In years past, we usually had heated discussions about when Christmas decorations would go up. We've compromised and have agreed to the last week of November or the first week of December.

While Gina loves Christmas, I'm not such a big fan. I don't know precisely what it is about Christmas, maybe it's that Gina is typically working (she's worked nine out of the last eleven Christmas days), or perhaps it's because I'm tired of accumulating stuff that I use for a couple of days or weeks—stuff that inevitably sits there cluttering the house. I used to love working during the Christmas holidays when I worked with folks who had developmental disabilities. Seeing their faces light up when you cooked them a special meal, brought them to their families' houses, or took them out to see Santa some-where around town.

I know I'm going to sound like an old man by saying this, but I just think that the focus of Christmas has lost its meaning. No, I'm not talking about the whole *Just put Christ back in Christmas!* Instead, Christmas for me has always meant gathering around people you love, sitting down with them, playing games with them, having a drink or two, and enjoying each other's presence. Though I will say that as the kids get older, I enjoy Christmas a little more. They're more into telling stories, playing games, and hanging out with every-one, so maybe there is still hope for me.

This year was different. There was no, "Hey Jay...let's put up the Christ-mas tree" discussions, and before I knew it, it was halfway through December, and we still hadn't put up the Christmas tree. Gina's maternity leave was just ending, so we were having discussions with her bosses at work and the doc-tors who would put her on sick leave so that she could continue processing her thoughts and feelings. Her job is such that she needs to be in control, and she deals with some crazy stuff. She needs to make sure that she's showing up in a centered way so that she can be in the best position to help folks that don't always want her there. She loves the job, so taking some additional time off after the initial maternity leave, which in my opinion was way too short, took some courage from her.

Almost a month after Ezra, Gina's cousin gave birth to a little boy, Harri-son, who was the exact same weight and length as our little Ezra. It was like a kick in the gut, yet we were over the moon for them. A little while later, we found ourselves in a church, readying ourselves to witness the baptism of this beautiful little guy.

We arrived later than we wanted and found ourselves sitting in the middle of the church, exactly where we didn't want to be. We were aiming to sit at the back, on the side, somewhere it would be easy for us to duck out if needed as the emotions got to us. We started the service strong, putting Zoey in the nursery and Carson between us. The first few songs went by, and the thoughts and emotions began to emerge for Gina. She left to walk through the halls and witness the baptism from the back doors of the church.

Then came the main event, the baptism. I sat there, clutching Carson on my lap, holding on to him for dear life. Matthew, the new dad, stood up and went to the pulpit. "As many of you know, we had some difficulty with Harrison when he was born; there were a couple of times during those first few days that we weren't sure we'd be able to take him home." He stopped to take a breath and looked up from his piece of paper. "So, I wanted to read a poem that you've probably heard of, that I think addresses how God held us through our experience." He looked up from his piece of paper and took another deep breath before continuing.

"It's called *Footsteps in the Sand*:

One night I dreamed a dream.
As I was walking along the beach with my Lord.
Across the dark sky flashed scenes from my life.
For each scene, I noticed two sets of footprints in the sand.
One belonged to me and one to my Lord.
After the last scene of my life flashed before me,
I looked back at the footprints in the sand.
I noticed that at many times along the path of my life,
Especially at the very lowest and saddest times,
There was only one set of footprints.
This really troubled me, so I asked the Lord about it.
"Lord, you said once I decided to follow you,
You'd walk with me all the way.
But I noticed that during the saddest and most troublesome times of my life,
There was only one set of footprints.
I don't understand why, when I needed You the most,
You would leave me."

He whispered, "My precious child, I love you and will never leave you,
Never, ever, during your trials and testings.
When you saw only one set of footprints,
It was then that I carried you."

I looked around the sanctuary and saw the people wiping tears from their eyes. I looked up to the pulpit and saw Matthew trying to keep himself composed as he finished the poem. I'm unsure what he said next; I was just trying to stay in my seat. I was filled with rage and anger; I wanted to jump out of my seat and run out of that sanctuary. Not because Matthew did anything or because of his experience either. That is simply not even close to my experience with God over the past few months. I wanted to yell at all those in the sanctuary and say, "Really? You think that's what it's like? Do you think that it's so nice and tidy like that? You experience difficulties, and God just cuddles you in and carries you across the difficult part of your life? Screw you and your stupid perfect image of God."

With every fiber in my body, I fought the urge and tried breathing into my own experience. Do people really experience this simple and tidy kind of God? Why has my experience been so different? Yes, absolutely, I have felt God's presence through all of this. I felt God as she wrapped her arms around me into a deep, tight bear hug. I've heard that God has said that she will never let me go and will always be there for me. But I have never come close to experiencing this idea of God picking me up, cuddling me into her bosom, and carrying me across the hot coals and dangers that lay there in the sand.

If anything, I have experienced God more as the sober friend at the party, draping my one arm over God's shoulder, and she weaved in and out of the people, stumbling alongside me, to tuck me into bed after a rough night. I've experienced God as the parent who tightly holds your little hand as you try and escape as you walk across the road. I've experienced God taking all my punches and kicks as violent thoughts and actions work their way through my toddler-sized body, and as I look up, I see God smiling warmly and saying, "I love you. I will never leave you." But picking me up and cuddling me in to walk me through the dark times, guarding me against potential dangers? That just hasn't been my experience. Yes, God has been there every step of the way, I've felt it, but God didn't shield me from all the dangers. God may have taken the brunt of it, but I certainly took some shots to the face throughout the whole process.

"Hey Jay, I'm just wondering...is there anything we can do this Christmas to honour Ezra? It doesn't have to be anything large, or anything like that; I just want to ensure that we provide the space to honour Ezra during our time together." This was the text my mom sent me.

Oh man, what does she have planned, I thought. My mom, bless her soul, has always been a planner. My dad has been the one who is perfectly comfortable with ambiguity, but my mom's idea of spontaneous fun was to have three planned-out games available for people to play without knowing which game people would pick at the time.

When I graduated from grade 8, my dad was given a choice in his job: move to the west coast of North America or take a good severance package. My dad decided he was tired of working for corporate America and that this was his opportunity to start a new journey, to work for himself. So, when I was about to graduate from elementary school, my mom and dad decided that this was going to be one of the only times in their lives that they would have so much freedom that they could take the family on a six-week vacation across the USA in our van and pop-up trailer.

So we packed up our full-sized blue and white GMC van, put the bicycles on the trailer, and left the house. We knew where our first destination was going to be but after that? All we knew is we wanted to hit a couple of cool sites like Yellowstone Park, Mount Rushmore, and the real purpose of the trip: the Grand Canyon. If my mom (or me at that time) had been in charge, there would have been a full itinerary for each day of the trip, how many kilometres would have to be driven each day, and deposits given to each campsite that we were going to be staying at. But my dad was the main planner for that trip, so, on any given day, we typically didn't know where we would stay from one night to the next or even what state we would be in.

I envy the courage that it would have taken my parents to leave with four children, the oldest in grade 8 and the youngest in grade 2 and arrive back home – 6 weeks later – with all four children. That's a lot of family time in a van and trailer.

I look back on that trip fondly. I learned a lot that trip about my family, setting up and taking down our trailer, some of the beautiful things that exist in our world, and how to deal with boredom. I also learned how beautiful it is to be spontaneous and roll with whatever life gives you. It was a trip that started to build my character in magnificent ways, and it seeped into my DNA.

So, when my mom sent me that message, I couldn't respond yet because I didn't know where we would be at around Christmas. So I simply replied, "I don't know yet, Mom; give me some time to think about it when it gets a little closer to the time."

It was a wonderful invitation to think about. What does it look like for us to honour Ezra's birth during Christmas? The time when we celebrate the birth of another individual who changed the course of history. An individual born into the world and who became a guiding light for so many. Sometimes I wonder, what would it have been like to be Jesus' parents?

Can you imagine what it would have been like to be Joseph or Mary and what disruption this would be to their lives? They were engaged to be married, and suddenly, this angel shows up to Mary's house and says, "Hey Mary... soooo... you're pregnant. Oh, also, you're going to give birth to this little guy that is going to be known as THE Saviour. Like...the Lord." Can you picture that conversation?

I wonder what Mary said to Joseph, "Hey hun...so I got a little visit from this ANGEL last night...and he said I was pregnant...I know, I know, we haven't even...you know...but that's what he told me!"

What do you think Joseph was thinking at that time? I can just picture him sitting there in his wood shop. *Yeah... I should probably break this off... but I don't want to hurt Mary; I love her deeply...I'll have to do this tactfully and quietly.* Then Joseph gets a visit from an angel. "Hey Jo, so there's this funny thing about God...he knows your thoughts, and we know you're planning on dumping Mary, but...you can't. You guys are being called to have this little baby boy. Oh, and... you're going to call him Jesus."

Can you imagine the disruption brought into the lives of Joseph and Mary? Two small-town lovers, engaged to be wed, ready to settle down in their little town and build their family. Then God says to them, "I have bigger plans for you. Plans for the Saviour to come to this world through your family."

I know that if it was me, I would have some pretty big questions to ask God. "Really, God? Me? And my soon-to-be-wife? You want us to bring the Saviour into this world? Why me? Why us? There's nothing special about us; how do you expect us to protect and nurture the freaking Saviour?"

I wonder if they looked back on their lives after Jesus was born, ministered, and then died on the cross and thought, *Whoa...that was crazy.* I know I would have. I think about little Ezra and think about some of the conversations I've had with God. Conversations like, "Okay, God, I'm assuming that you have a plan with all of this, I trust this, but really...is there no other way? Couldn't we do this through another avenue? I wouldn't wish this type of experience on my worst enemy, but does it really have to be me? Us? Could you at least tell me what the plan is? That would make it a little easier to trust. If you could just tell me the end goal, that would be great. If I could just see what the point of all of this is, I can deal with the difficulties of the present."

So, what did it mean for us to honour Ezra at Christmas? I had no idea.

Gina and I talked about it, and we wanted to ensure that nothing big was done. It was still too fresh, too raw for us to spend a Christmas celebration honouring our dead son. Sure, if it were just us, that would be a different experience, but Ezra's brother and sister would be there, and all my sisters and their husbands would be there. We didn't need and didn't want everyone to spend their Christmas down in the dumps, sifting through the shit that grief and loss bring. That didn't sound like a good Christmas.

CHAPTER 7

Big News!

JANUARY 2017

When we lost Ezra, we received a slew of different reactions from people. Some were great interactions, others, not so much. It got me thinking about Goldilocks (stick with me here). You know the story; Goldilocks walks into an empty house and tries a bit of the three bowls lying on the kitchen table. "Ouch!" she said, "this one is far too hot! My mouth is burning!" The second bowl was equally shocking. "Ugh...this one is too cold! I might as well suck on an ice cube!" Then she tried the third, "Ahhhh, yes...this hits the spot, it's just right."

Over the past few months Gina, and I have had our fair share of different reactions to our "news." We have had people who swooped in and burned our mouths, people who have disappeared from our lives and left behind a cold and clammy taste in our mouths, and still others who left a satisfying and nourishing taste. All those people meant well, I'm sure of it. I've started to think of it as kind of a Goldilocks effect.

One reaction was that of an acquaintance who was like the too-hot porridge. She swooped in like a hurricane; her energy threatened to entirely gulp us up and sweep us off our feet. She didn't read the social cues, how it made us uncomfortable, or how there was terror in our eyes.

"Oh, my goodness, I'm so sorry to hear about everything that you had to go through; I can't imagine what that's like; it must be so hard, so painful, so..." Tears streamed down her face, her mouth grasped for air, shoulders heaved up and down as she tried not to spiral completely out of control.

The hurricane cares only about itself at that moment. The person's emotions get so caught up with them that they lose sight of the people standing right in front of them. It creeps in from their peripherals and quickly becomes their primary focus, while everything else that existed, including the people in front of them, fades into the background. They can't handle the silence that often comes with grief, so they fill each silence with every word they can find in their word bank, speaking each one except the ones that actually have any meaning. They get so caught up in their emotions that the griever becomes the comforter while the hurricane becomes the griever. "There, there," the griever-turned-comforter will say, "It's okay; we'll get through this."

Then some responded quite differently. In many cases, their response was to offer no response. The cold porridge they offer causes your mouth to turn sour, and you forcefully gulp down your bite. They are like an ostrich, burying their head in the earth to avoid any contact. They'll go through the whole workday without discussing "it." They actively avoid the subject that you are grieving, not knowing that everything they talk about reminds you of your grief. This was the case of a co-worker whom I had worked with. I spent the entire day with her, listening to her talk and complain about her kids, waiting for her to acknowledge me or that I had just lost my son a couple of weeks prior. But there was nothing—no mention of anything.

The ostrich works under the pretense that less is more, so they do the least amount of "comforting" possible. Mostly, I think they do this out of good reasoning. I know I've found myself there as well. "Well, I don't want to remind them of their loss. They probably just want to get their work done today." In the meantime, the griever sits in agony, saying, "Everything around me reminds me of my grief, all of the life that surrounds me. Anything you say can't be worse than not saying anything at all!"

Their avoidance, whether perceived or real, seems to symbolize that you are, in some way, contagious. If they talk, it feels like they may also get caught in the disease of grief, and that thought is unbearable. The worst thing, though, that the ostrich does is give the "sad eyes" without saying a word. It's not empathy; it's not sympathy; it's more like pity. "You poor soul, I can't believe you fell for love's tricks." You know they know. They know they know. Yet, putting our heads in the sand is more manageable than opening Pandora's box. Ostriches come in all genders, all shapes, and all sizes. Their lack of acknowledgment strikes you right to the core: "I'm right here! You can see me! I exist, and my pain exists as well!"

Then some are just right. It has nothing to do with what they say because they don't know the right words either. They don't necessarily do the "right" things, but their presence, in and of itself, is comfort. It's not because you've known them for a while or because they are a stranger. It's because they let you be. They say things like "I'm sorry for your loss" or better yet, "I have no clue what to say," and then sit in the silence, letting you define what you need from them. When my friend Benji showed up at the hospital, he rushed into our room, grabbed me by the shoulders, and brought me in for the biggest hug I've ever received. He whispered through his tears, "Jay, I'm so sorry, I... I just don't know what to say, but I love you, and am here for you."

Then he let me go and sat in silence, just being a presence. That presence meant all the world to me.

These people show up in many different forms: with flowers on the coffee table, cards that litter the counter, meals they prepare, and the random text message that says, "Thinking of you." They don't claim to know the answers, the right things to say, the right thing to do, and they don't need to.

Some expel tears and sobs, others are stoic, but what makes these people special is that they are there. Fully there. Their presence is completely and utterly in the room. They sit with you even though it's uncomfortable; they empathize with you even though it forces them to feel their past experiences. They sit in the shit and don't plug their nose. They simply be. Outwardly, there is nothing special about these people, but inwardly these are the folks willing to sit through the tears, laughter, hopes, and defeat even though the experience is likely to change them. They are courageous enough to listen to our stories even though they cannot be unheard.

I wonder if it's because the stories of grief and loss hit us right at our very core. There are reasons why all three types of people respond the way they do, and I can't help but think it's because of our core. Some of us have done more work in that area than others. I've learned from all these types of people, and one of the lessons is that we all need to work on ourselves. The more that we do that, the more we can enter someone else's story and simply be.

I know there have been times when I have shown up in all three positions in others' lives. There've been times when I robbed someone of their chance to grieve, times when I've ignored the pain of someone's loss, and times when I've genuinely shown up. And in this realization, I promise to be there for others. I will show up and say, "This sucks, and I'm here to love you in whatever way you need."

Too often, we show up and tell people, "Don't worry, it will get better; time heals all." And maybe it will. But perhaps it won't. That's not showing up; that's robbing the person of the love they deserve. At that moment, the person cries out to be loved, have someone listen to their story, or even sit with them simply to be with them, giving them the space to sit in the shit pile. When we say, "Don't worry, things will get better," what we are really saying is, "Push all those feelings way down; you're not actually feeling those feelings; get over yourself. You don't need them, and one day, you'll see, you'll be just fine." We see the love they express for another and take it. We steal it right in front of them. All anyone is looking for is to be loved and to love.

One of my family's traditions is to get together with my Mom's side of the family every Christmas. Usually, it's a bit of a mess, with family coming from Alberta, Grand Rapids, Huntsville, and then more local places, where my grandparents live. Everyone brings something. A potato dish, ribs, jerk chicken, and salads; the food begins to pile high on the table.

Christmas had left me feeling raw and emotional, and another Christmas event at the beginning of January wasn't helping. It was the first time I would see some of my aunts, uncles, and cousins since we lost Ezra, and he was a topic that would come up. I'm grateful, really; it would be much more difficult if nobody mentioned a thing, but still difficult nonetheless.

On our way home from our family Christmas get-together Gina said, "So...I'm feeling a little off. Why don't you drop me and the kids off at home and go grab a pregnancy test."

"Uh, what?" I responded. I was more than a little shocked. With our first child, Carson, I don't think we even had sex; I just looked at her the right way, and BAM – pregnant. With our second, Zoey, the whole "process" took a little longer, a few months or so. With Ezra, we were about a month or two away from getting tested to see if something was keeping Gina from getting pregnant. Our expectations for another child were for the future, not this quickly.

So, I brought home the pregnancy tests as requested, and moments later we found out Gina was pregnant. "Oh, this is going to be a crappy and wonderful nine months," Gina said. All I could do was nod through my tears. Knowing that we would need the support over the next few months that we were supposed to keep this news a "secret," we decided to tell our closest friends the news. Typically, I had always been bad at keeping those secrets. This time, however, there was no way that I wanted to tell people we were expecting another addition only to have a miscarriage in the first trimester.

The next day, I went to visit Ezra at his grave. I had been going once every couple of weeks. I would sit there, I would chat with him, I would cry, and I would sit in his and God's presence and pray.

That morning I stood there looking at the cross my Opa had made for us, a large white cross with a smaller wood-coloured cross on the front with the words Ezra William Dykstra stretched out across the smaller cross. Each letter was etched into the wood by my Opa's careful and caring hands. Underneath Ezra's name, in slightly smaller writing, it said, "Safely in Jesus' Arms."

Everything started as it usually does; I would crouch down so that I was eye-level with the writing, then slowly trace my fingers over each letter as tears would start to flow down my cheeks. I started to pray, "God, this sucks; this really sucks, why couldn't he be here with us. Why couldn't I hold him in my arms for days, weeks, months, even longer. Oh God, I know that you have wisdom in all of this; sometimes I just...I just have a hard time accepting it. But God, I trust in you, I trust in your wisdom, I trust in your love; this just sucks."

I started to update Ezra about what was happening in our lives, but when it came to telling him about the new baby in Mommy's tummy, I broke down. I slumped to the cold, damp ground, knees right into hardened grass, and said, "Oh buddy, I don't know how to say this, we just love you so much, and we so wish you were here...you're going to have another sibling...oh God, our table just isn't full yet, we're not trying to replace you, buddy, nothing, nobody, can replace you. I'm not trying to make excuses, and I know you understand better than even I do; nothing can replace you. Nothing. Nobody. Oh God, I love you so much, and oh shit...this hurts so fucking much."

I looked up at the cloud-covered sky as the sun started to break through. I sat there, slumped in the grass, watching the transition as the sun shone and beamed down on me. Then, a bird flew by, perched on a tombstone nearby, and sang a song to comfort me. I knew, at that moment, that Ezra and God were there, smiling a blessing down on me, saying, "You are a beloved child of God, and this new one will also be loved more than you can ever imagine."

CHAPTER 8

The Return of the Dad-Hat

FEBRUARY 2017

The beginning of February marked a significant shift from the past six months for us. Gina was going back to work. She had been off for the last six months and felt it was time to return to work. This meant a significant shift to how we ran our household would exist. I would have to put my dad's cap back on for the next while.

Gina was nervous and excited to return to work, and I was getting increasingly nervous as the day grew closer. Since Gina works shifts, the last six months had slightly differed from how we typically operate. One of the nice parts about Gina being a shift worker and me being self-employed is that the self-employed person works around the shift worker's schedule. That way, we can minimize things like daycare. The nice part about the shift worker being off work is the self-employed person just works because there are limited reasons why he can't work that much more.

And then, when that shift worker returns to work, the self-employed person has to start watching the kids more and adjusting their schedule to make sure that everyone is where they need to be without falling through the cracks. So, as you can imagine, I'm a little nervous on a few fronts.

For starters, the colour-coded calendar. Our lives quite literally revolve around our calendar. If it's not in the calendar, then it's not happening. It's all colour coded so that a quick glance gives you a good picture of what's happening that week. For example, a few weeks ago, I was supposed to go out for drinks with a friend, but I didn't put it on the calendar for whatever reason. Guess who wasn't ready when that friend came to pick me up?

Truth be told, I'm not always great at remembering, even if it's on the calendar, especially if it doesn't directly involve me. Not long ago, I got the kids ready for the day because Gina was at work. I fed them breakfast, and Carson started getting his backpack ready so he could go to school. I loaded up the kids in the car and drove the few minutes down the road to the school. Only the school was eerily quiet. There weren't any cars around dropping off their children, the buses were nowhere to be found, and no kids were playing on the playground. I looked at the clock on my car, thinking that we were late to school, only to see we were right on time. As we sat in the car in front of the school, I grilled Carson about why no one else was there.

Then I looked up and saw the school sign...where it clearly said today was a P.A. Day. "Why didn't I put that in the calendar?" I said to myself as I pulled out my phone, only to find it in green on the calendar.

I'm really nervous about altered routines. The kids, my wife, and me—we're all in some solid routines at this moment. In a few days that all shifts, and we become inconsistently consistent with our shift-working schedule. Yes, we live by our calendar, but shift work doesn't allow for you to have a constant routine, never mind the effects it has on kids. That's one thing that nobody tells you when you sign up for shift work. It's not just you working it. Your whole family has to adjust to that schedule. The last six months have been nice because we've been able to have set times to go to the gym every week, have a normal supper time, and have an evening routine that we could generally stick to. Of course, we try to have some consistent routines in our house, but the person implementing that routine is not always the same person, and each person brings their own flare to the job.

And truth be told, I'm nervous about being a dad again. Sure, I've been a dad over the last six months, but now I must be "on" way more than the previous half-year. It almost feels like you've been sitting on the sidelines for so long watching the game take place that you forget what it's like to be a starter on the court. Having the whole team rely on you as you take the final shot. I've been active over the last six months, but truthfully, I've probably been more on the sidelines because I'm the one who gets to leave the house and go to work.

So, what does this all mean for me?

Well, it means I have to do more cooking, more cleaning, and more time with the kiddos, which will allow us to have more adventures.

I'm also a little worried about how Gina will react to returning to work. I know it will be good for her to start putting other things in her mind, but I'm nervous. The one comforting thing is that she won't be able to go back on the road. Once the service finds out you're pregnant, you get chained to a desk so that your risks of something happening to the baby are decreased, and it probably also has something to do with their liability.

Gina's work had been helpful to us, and I admired their honesty. They had come to visit us a little while ago, and as we sat around our table, the officer said, "Gina, Jay...I'll be honest, I don't know what to say." The police force that Gina is on is a smaller one, and there aren't many women serving there. As a result, this was something new for them as well.

It surprised me that the officer came in, sat at our table, and opened with, "I don't know what to say." I don't know what I had expected, but I know it wasn't that. He sat with us for a while, checking in to ensure we were doing alright. It's one of the wonderful sides of the police force, or emergency services in general that people don't talk too often about. It used to be called the "brotherhood," though I'm not sure that term still rings as true. It's this idea that we're all struggling when one of us is struggling. You see it, especially at police funerals. I remember a while back, an officer down in the US passed away, and he was related to an officer whom Gina works with. Gina was one of the first to help organize a van of officers from her station to make the long trek down to the funeral so that they could support their brother in blue. There's something about a community willing to be present through some of the worst moments in a fellow officer's life.

It's interesting having a police officer as a spouse. You get some interesting questions. One of my favourites is that women often approach me and say, "I don't think I could ever be married to a police officer. I would be worried all the time! I'd be so afraid that something would happen to them. Don't you ever worry about your wife?"

Honestly, I do worry sometimes. Not because I think she'll put herself in a dangerous situation, although…that's kind of her job sometimes. But people are unpredictable, and she deals with folks who aren't always in the best place of their lives. Regardless my response to these women is that yes, it can be a dangerous job, but she loves serving where she's at, and I'm behind her one hundred percent.

Probably the most interesting part about being a police officer's spouse is that at police functions, all the guys are talking about their experiences, and their wives and partners have their own side conversations. I don't have experience kicking down doors or chasing people, and since I'm not a female, I don't really fit in with the wives either. So, if I start talking to the wives, I start to get side glances from their partners, and I don't have much to contribute to a conversation about the latest police events that have taken place, so I usually sit there and observe.

It's actually one of my favourite pastimes—sitting and observing, It's one of the reasons I love airports and coffee shops; there are always people to watch. It's fun to see how they interact with each other, and how they deal with stress, how they see the world around them. Sitting in on my fair share of police parties and events, I've had the chance to watch a lot of different interactions and meet a lot of great people—people who serve their community by keeping them safe, enforcing rules, and helping people find their way out of a rut.

Then there are the others. The stereotypical Type-A personality that needs to one-up each story, drink the extra beer, and be the centre of attention. One thing I've learned about men in my life is that the louder and more offensive they are, the more they're typically hurting on the inside. When Gina first got in as a police officer, I was a little more bitter, and I used to hate these types of guys. I didn't like the way they talked, what they talked about, and how I was always ignored. I was also a lot more self-conscious then and never felt like I measured up to these guys, if I'm being honest. I always felt like less of a man when I was in their presence because I didn't know how to shoot a gun, fight, or be tough. But as I've grown, I've come to realize that those are all masks—masks they put on each day to protect themselves from being who they really are. It's a front to hide the brokenness, the vulnerability, and the hurt that exists deep within them.

As a male spouse of a police officer, you start to see some of the injustices within the system that (typically) white men have set up. Injustices about how women are still treated in a predominantly male environment, how women are seen, or not seen, in these systems, but that's not really my story to share.

As the spouse of a police officer, it's an honour to support someone who is serving her community and her country. It's an honour to watch your spouse go to work, day in and day out to serve their community. It's an honour to be a part of the "personhood" that exists in the emergency service world. When one aches, the community aches alongside them.

CHAPTER 9

For The Love of Control

MARCH 2017

M y sister had it all planned out. She and her husband-to-be were going to have an outdoor wedding. They had the location all picked out; it was a beautiful spot that overlooked a small river and was picture-perfect. They planned to have a tent set up just up the hill from the spot where they were going to exchange vows, but let's be honest, the tent was plan Z.

On the day of the wedding, much to my sister's dismay, and despite all the prayers she lifted up leading up to that day, it rained. Not just a light sprinkle either; it poured. So, all her guests stood under the tent and waited. We sat there for a long time, waiting and waiting for the rain to stop. Only it didn't. We tried to coerce mother nature into stopping the rain, putting all our mental capacities to work and willing it to stop, but it kept raining. Finally, there was a moment when the rain slowed to a mere pitter-patter, gently sprinkling our heads, so my sister decided that was good enough, and they went out in the rain and got hitched.

I think we all love control. We love controlling our feelings, thoughts, other people, jobs, and schedules. We especially love to control what happens to us. That day, though, at my sister's wedding, we could not control the rain.

I've been reading Richard Rohr a lot lately, and he defines suffering as whenever we are not in control. He also says that we must go down before we can go up. In other words, suffering is a necessary experience for us to experience the growth of our True self. In one of his daily meditations that end up in my inbox every morning, Rohr writes, "Suffering is the most effective way whereby humans learn to trust, allow, and give up control to Another Source."

There's only one major problem. We love control.

When Gina was pregnant with Ezra, we loved to play the control game. We would dream of the things we would teach him, where he would sleep, how our other two children would react and interact, and the vacations we would take during maternity leave. My kids and I would do math using Ezra as our math problem – when Ezra turns three, how old will Zoey be? Carson? We had it all planned out because we were in control.

And then life happens. It takes our neatly planned life, curls it into a ball, and hits us repeatedly with a baseball bat. It sucker-punches us in the stomach and round-house kicks us in the head when we're crouched over, gasping for breath. It drags us kicking and screaming into this shit-storm that we call suffering—life out of control.

It's fitting I'm thinking about control as it's Holy Week in the church. The week that leads up to Good Friday. The name "Good Friday" has always struck me as a little weird. After all, it's the day that Jesus was flogged, spit at, mocked, and nailed to a freaking cross. It doesn't seem like a very good Friday to me. I'm sure Jesus wasn't ecstatic about it either; he even asked God, "Are you sure we want to do this? Because if there's another way around all of this, that would be pretty great..."

When Jesus died on the cross, the story is that the earth went black, and the temple curtain was torn from top to bottom. The earth shook violently, and rocks of the earth split. The earth shook so violently that bodies rose from the ground and entered the cities. The first zombie apocalypse.

Now, I'm no theologian, but I wonder if this was God's mourning. I wonder if God was tearing his clothes, turning off the lights, and falling into her bed sobbing over the loss of God's son. The one and only son that God sent to earth. Being taken to his knees by the sheer feeling of being overwhelmed that grief often brings. Reaching for a tissue because the tears clogged up her nose.

In churches, it's been my experience that we are very uncomfortable with Good Friday. We try our best to have a solemn experience and to be like mourners going to a funeral service, but we can't help but put an asterisk at the end of the service: "Don't forget to come back on Sunday when Jesus rises from the dead!"

On Good Friday morning, I went to church alone. Gina decided she couldn't do church that day, but I knew that one of our friends had worked hard on the service, and I wanted to make sure I was there to support her. I came in a little late and grabbed my spot at the back of the church.

There's something about sitting in the back that I enjoy. You can see everything happening in front of you, and you get the best view of everything. Maybe it's another control thing; I don't like sitting in the middle or the front because there is so much potentially happening behind me that it makes it hard for me to focus. I like to think it's because I like to watch people.

Regardless, I grabbed my seat in the back and settled in for a sombre service. Many in the church wore black, the symbol of mourning, and the pastor was up front giving the message. Typically, our church services end, and everyone chats on their way out about how their weekend was going before heading downstairs to the gym to grab some coffee. This service was a little different, though. There was a wheelbarrow in the front, and we were given a stone when we first arrived. At the end of the service, everyone went up one side of the aisle, across the front of the church, placed their rock in the wheelbarrow, and exited down the other aisle. All in silence.

I stood in line going down the aisle, listening to people throw their rock in the wheelbarrow. *Boom, boom, boom,* went the rocks. I watched how uncomfortable people were in dealing with death, uncertainty, and the pain of hearing the sounds of the rocks hitting the bottom of the wheelbarrow. Some people walked as quickly as they could out of the sanctuary so that they could start talking again. Others couldn't help themselves and talked back and forth anyway. Others still tried to feel comfortable in the silence, but their face and body expressions told a different story.

In the front of the church sat my friend. She sat there, her eyes closed, feeling every rock hit the wheelbarrow.

There's something eerie about being in a group of people when all is silent. It's so eerie it freaks people out, but I love it. It's an absolutely beautiful sound. The sound of no sound. You can hear the slight shuffling of feet, the occasional cough or sniffle, and the sound of clothing material rubbing together. In the breaks of those little noises is a beautiful silence. One honouring of God.

We're uncomfortable with grief, suffering, and the loss of control. We want to bypass Jesus hanging on the cross and go straight to his resurrection.

"Yeah, yeah, I know Jesus died, but he also rose; why don't we just talk about that," we say. We do this outside church as well. We're often scared even to ask grieving people, "How are you doing?" because we're scared their answer is going to be truthful, and we're not sure if we can handle their truth. So, we try to make them feel better; we try to cheer them up.

That's not the world we live in, though. We're surrounded by suffering. We are surrounded by grief. We're surrounded by people losing control. Every day is Good Friday.

Turn on the news, and you'll find some treacherous murder that has taken place. Scroll through your social media and look at the social injustices occurring across our world. Turn on the radio and hear the news anchor tell of another suicide.

We are surrounded, and every day is Good Friday.

So maybe, I thought, just maybe, we need to bask in the learning of Good Friday. Maybe, just maybe, we need to sit in the pain, the suffering, and the grief. Maybe there is learning for us there. Maybe there is transformation there. Maybe through our pain comes new life.

Maybe the journey down through our pain and suffering is the way we rise.

A few weeks later, I sat in my therapist's office. "So, I realized something during Easter," I started saying. "These last few months, I've been doing what you told me. I've been sitting in the shit. Look at what all exists around me, accepting the invitation to enter into the pain, the suffering, the grief, but I forgot a pivotal thing you said."

"And what's that, Jason?" my therapist asked.

"I was so attentive to sitting with the pain that I forgot to let it go! That's what we talked about last time, right? Sitting with the pain, acknowledging it, and then letting it go."

"Yes, that's what we talked about. Tell me a little more about your experience with this. What exactly did you 'forget' to let go of?"

As we talked back and forth, I realized I had forgotten to let go of my ego. My ego was getting in the way of discovering my true self and mining the lessons from Ezra. My ego was standing in the way of me accepting others' help. I had made my life about helping other people, but there was something too risky about being the person who was being helped.

A few years ago, I was driving my motorcycle home in October. It looked like the last ride of the season with cooler temperatures rushing in, and I had just gotten new glasses. I decided to take the bike for one more spin. On the way home, I followed a truck that started slowing down and put on its turn signal to turn right. As the truck slowly moved into the turning lane, I began to speed up to go past it, but when I got right beside it, in front of me was the driver-side of a blue Ford Edge staring right at me. The driver of the vehicle must have seen the truck turning right onto the road where they were sitting and didn't see anybody behind them, so they made the rush decision to turn left...right in front of me. I laid the bike down and must have kicked off it because it slid underneath her vehicle, and I slid right around the Edge.

It all happened so fast. The next thing I knew, I was standing in the middle of the road thinking, *oh man, I should get out of the road; I'm going to get hit!* So, I walked to the side of the road while the driver pulled over to the other side. A few cars stopped, and I pulled out my phone to call Gina.

"Hey...Gina...I'm okay, but you should know I just got into a motorcycle accident...yes, I'm okay...I'm standing at the side of the road...could you come pick me up? Oh, and we'll need to let Jesse and Russ know and get them to bring their truck... we'll need to get this bike out of here before the cops arrive."

I don't know why I was frightened of the cops at that instant. I had probably said that phrase too many times in my youth when we were riding around quads and dirt bikes.

Gina was six months pregnant at the time, so she wasn't overly impressed with the lady who caused the accident. I went to the hospital and was thankful that I only had some severe road rash, even though I wore all my safety gear.

For the next few weeks, Gina would come home on her breaks from work to re-bandage me. I was quite hesitant to have her, or anyone else for that matter, come to help. There was something about asking and receiving help that has always left me feeling too vulnerable, almost as if I was walking around town naked or something.

I had made a life for myself where I was always the helper. I was the one there providing the support, the food, the assistance; I was the helper. But the helper wasn't supposed to need help; were they?

There's something about receiving help that leaves us with this vulnerability. It's as if we've been told to strip down all our clothes and stand in front of a crowd. It's kind of weird. At the same moment, there is this feeling of intense gratitude that someone cares enough to assist you.

When Ezra was delivered, I got very good at saying, "Thanks for offering to help; at the time, we don't need anything, but I'll let you know if and when we do need something." Then I would file that information away for later and continue on with life.

So, what about asking for and receiving help that leaves us bare for all to see? Is it precisely that each word we offer when we ask for or accept help equivalent to taking off a piece of clothing?

Can (there goes your shirt) you (pants are off) help (there goes your underwear) me? And then you stand there naked and afraid...vulnerable. *What if they judge me? What if they see that I can't actually help them out right now? What if they see me in my weakness? What if I break down in front of them? What if I can never repay them?*

What if... We think...*What if...***What if they see the real me?** That's what we're scared of. What will happen if you see the real me? What if you see all my beauty marks and imperfections? What if you see all the scars and wounds? What if you see all the places of my life that are gluttonous?

That's the difficult part, and that's exactly why asking for help is not weakness. Asking for help is not a weakness; it's exposing our weakness, allowing ourselves to be vulnerable with another, and putting it out there. It's being honest about where you are at that moment. It's accepting others' generosity when you have nothing to offer. It's being willing to have your feet washed, not because you deserve it, but because you are loved.

Remember when Jesus tried to wash Peter's feet, and Peter said, "No! Jesus! You'll never wash my feet! You can't do that...I can't accept your help."

Then Jesus said to him, "Unless I wash you, you won't belong to me."

Peter replied, "Fine, Jesus, then don't stop at my feet, wash my head and hands as well!"

Peter didn't like accepting help either, especially from his teacher, his master, the one he loved so much. Peter was used to going out with Jesus and ministering to others, but when it came time for him to be helped, to be ministered to, it was a tough pill for Peter to swallow.

When Ezra was delivered, we got rocked. One of our friends would text us every time she left the house to run errands: "Hey guys...I'm just running to the grocery store; need anything?"

Every time we would reply, "Thanks, but we're good right now." Then she began texting us, "Hey you guys hungry? You want me to drop off some food tomorrow?" Every time we would reply, "Thanks, but we're good right now."

Despite everything happening, I still thought we didn't need help. I didn't feel that I deserved to be the recipient of help. I didn't want to enter that vulnerable state. I wanted to stay in control, and control of my surroundings, control of my feelings, and control of my future. I didn't want to feel that vulnerable with another person for fear of how I would break down.

But our friend didn't take no for an answer. She knew that we needed help; she could read it all over us, so soon the messages changed from "Hey, you guys hungry?" to "Hey, I just dropped off some food on your front step."

We had nothing to offer her, nothing to give her. We didn't earn the right to eat that food; we didn't work for it, pay for it, or promise to give something in return. We were brought food simply because we were being loved. So instead of saying no for weeks on end, I would gather up my courage and strength and make the conscious choice to open our door, stand there exposed for being someone in need, and accept a meal. And I would say, "Thank you for loving us."

CHAPTER 10

The Baby Whisperer

APRIL 2017

At the start of April, there were a lot of pregnant women in my life. Gina was pregnant, and our sister-in-law, Megan, was pregnant and due in April. Gina's sister Mandy was pregnant and due in May, and my sister Rachel was pregnant and due in July. It was like a baby apocalypse.

Both Megan and Mandy had given us a heads-up when they found out they were pregnant; they knew the news could shake us up. When Megan was ready, she found out the sex of the baby (They were going to have a boy!).

Our kids were beyond excited about all the upcoming babies. They would double their cousin count in just a few short months!

I didn't overthink all the upcoming babies. I think there was an expectation that a new baby would remind us of Ezra, and yeah, babies always remind me of Ezra, but that's not a problem. That's life.

The first time I saw a baby in the hospital after Ezra was for our friends Russ and Melissa. They had just had their fourth child, and I was sweating walking up to the hospital doors, even though it was the end of December.

My stomach all in knots. Anxiety pumping through my body. I walked into their hospital room, hugged them, and looked at the little baby girl in the bassinet. I don't quite know what I expected, but I do know that I expected it to be complex. I expected tears, more anxiety, and something major to occur. Nothing happened. The only thing I remember is looking at this beautiful baby girl and being so incredibly happy for my friends.

It's an amazing experience seeing your friends in the hospital having a baby. We have a close group of friends, and we're like any other dysfunctional family. All our kids love seeing each other, playing, and hanging out together. They already get in a lot of trouble together, and I'm sure that will continue as they get older. The most special and honourable thing for me was that when my friends started having their children, Gina and I got the special title of Aunt and Uncle. Anytime I hear one of those little children yell out, "Uncle Jay!!" it's a blessing I will always cherish.

Partway into April, Megan had her baby. A baby boy named Arie. The day Arie was born, I went to the hospital after work with some trepidation. Gina had already been to visit them, and she told me that it was hard. It was the first baby boy born into our inner circle since Ezra, and Gina had told me earlier that day that it was a difficult visit because it evoked so many different emotions; emotions of intense happiness for her brother and sister-in-law and a deep sadness about missing her baby boy.

I made my way through the hospital, and eventually found their room. They had a private room that looked more like a hotel room than it did a hospital room. I knocked on the door as I walked in. "Hello?" I squeaked out.

"Hey Jay! How are you doing?" Megan said.

Will was on the bed watching the basketball game on his iPad; Megan sat next to him, and little Arie was on the bed.

I replied, "I'm doing well. It's been a bit of a crazy day at work! But I'm here now! Congrats to you both on little Arie! How's the little guy doing?"

"Thanks, Jay," Megan said. "He's a little fussy and has been for the last few hours." She quickly changed his diaper and re-swaddled him as she talked. She picked him up, walked him over to me and put him in my arms.

It was everything I could do not to jump out of my skin. I have this rule about babies. As I mentioned, I don't hold them unless they can lift their own head, and I especially didn't want to hold Arie at that moment; I still hadn't figured out if I felt safe enough to do so. Megan could see the fear in my eyes, but she took the swaddled baby and placed him in my arms anyway. Sweat began to pour, and I was instantly glad that I hadn't taken off my coat yet so they couldn't see my physical reaction to all of this.

I looked down at the baby in my arms as I swayed back and forth. I flashbacked to holding Ezra at the hospital, swaddled and in my arms, rocking back and forth as to calm him, but knowing I was seeking to calm myself. At that moment, there were too many feelings to place them all. There was this deep fear that something would happen to this child, as if I was some virus and shouldn't be trusted around a child. There was this deep sadness and guilt for holding this little boy, almost feeling like I was cheating on Ezra with Arie. But mostly, I felt a deep love for this child, a desire to be the best possible uncle for this little one.

As I swayed back and forth, holding Arie, and talking with Will and Megan, all those difficult feelings began to wash away. The sweaty, clammy feeling started to subside, and I began to look at Arie a little differently. He wasn't Ezra; he was another beloved child of God. As I poured love onto him, he started to quiet and fall asleep. Megan was happy. "Looks like you can't leave now, Uncle Jay; you'll have to stay with us for the next few days to be our baby whisperer."

I smiled at them, looked down at Arie, and smiled brightly at him.

CHAPTER 11

What Brings You Hope?

MAY 2017

After starting The Shit Club and talking with folks, I began to get a question from all types of individuals. "Amidst all of this, what brings your family hope?"

It's a fair question, although a rather bold one, usually I try to answer. Whenever I do, my mind immediately shoots back to my youth, and I'm sitting in a classroom in the church basement. I typically sat beside Kyle and Jon, and it's probably safe to say that I was one of the talkative and challenging ones in the classroom.

I had mixed feelings about being in that church basement (or any classroom, for that matter). I loved seeing and chatting with my friends and learning but despised classrooms. However, this classroom was a little different than your typical school classroom. All of us kids were there (read: forced by parents) to learn more about the Bible and God. We often had to do memory work which consisted of Bible verses or pieces of the catechism. One piece of memory work has never left me. It's Lord's Day 1 of the Heidelberg Catechism, which says,

Question: What is your only comfort in life and in death?

Answer: That I am not my own, but belong—body and soul, in life and in death—to my faithful Saviour Jesus Christ. He has fully paid for all my sins with his precious blood and has set me free from the tyranny of the devil.

Alright, that's all I remember. I know there's more to the answer, but that's all that stuck. When someone asks me, "What brings your family hope?" this plays through my mind. God. Jesus. The Holy Spirit. It is what brings me peace and hope. It's the comfort of knowing that I belong to my Savior in life and death.

This question of hope is quite a loaded question. It's one of those questions that goes to the depths of a person. It's a question of resilience, the core of enabling and empowering you. What allows you to move forward when you are wading through the shit waist deep.

Does this mean I'm always at peace? Ha...seriously! I'm trying to stop laughing over here.

Sometimes my mind is so clouded in sadness, loss, suffering, breakdowns, depression, and self-loathing that I can barely feel the ground. It's part of the journey, though. There will be dark times. There will be times spent in a Zen-like garden in the clouds. There will be everything in between. More often than not, I think it's holding the tension between the two.

Holding the tension between this dark lake of despair and the cloudy Zen garden. If we only go to the depths of the lake of despair, we end up so clouded by our hurt, our pain, our sadness, guilt, shame, pity, and thoughts that we can never actually return. If we only go to the heights of the cloudy Zen garden, we end up with a false reality that everything is rosy and peaceful and that there is no such thing as suffering or hurt. We become blind to the reality that surrounds us. So, we hold these two in an ongoing tension. The knowledge that we also have hope and experience God's love enables us to enter the depths of Lake Despair. It gives us the safety of a hand that guides us, holds us close, and keeps us safe.

Living in the tension gives us permission to sit and honour each – despair and hope – sometimes at the same time. From a spiritual side, knowing I am not my own helps me live with that tension. It helps me live into despair and hope knowing that I'm not the only one on this journey. That there's a light-house ahead of me, showing me that love is the reason for this pain and the way through.

Then there's the community that surrounds us. Those people that show up in the wonderful and the sadness. Those that celebrate with us and those that mourn with us. The people that show up not just for the good moments but for the difficult and shitty moments. I'm one of those people that hate to depend on others for pretty much anything, which is funny because I love to help others. For whatever reason, I hate asking for help. I'll try my best to deal with a situation independently, often to my detriment. And yet, we aren't hardwired to do this life alone, so when our community shows up and journeys alongside us in each of those interactions, there's a glimmer of hope. When things get tough, our tears fog up our glasses, making it difficult to see anything past our noses and challenging us to take the next step... When we have one or two people by our side, though, they can whip out their lens cleaner and gently caress those foggy lenses so that we can continue to put one foot in front of the other. Sure, the lens may still be smudged, but we can start to see the ground beneath us. With each stop-in, text, and conversation, the community around us pours out their love when we can't generate any of our own. It's through that love that sustains us, that carries us when we cannot carry ourselves.

Lastly, there's something about being insignificant; by that, I don't mean unimportant. You'll know what I mean if you've ever been to the mountains. The first time my wife and I travelled to the mountains was in Alberta, and we were in complete awe. We'd leave the car at every pull-over available and stand there in silence as our brains tried to comprehend the beauty in front of us. At one such stop, Gina said, "Doesn't it make you feel so insignificant?" There's something about being a small fish in a big pond. There's something incredible about knowing that we're not entirely in control of everything. There is something about not being able to influence a situation. There is something about being insignificant. Regardless of all my power and influence, I can not control the fact that we have lost our son. Of all my abilities to change my situation, I cannot bring Ezra back to life. It doesn't matter how hard I try or wish for the outcome to be different; it will not bring about a different outcome. I'm just not that powerful, and there's something comforting in that. Instead of trying to control all the things that are wildly out of my control, I can start to surrender to what life gives me in those moments. That means I can start focusing on giving myself grace and compassion. Pouring out the deserved love for myself, even when I don't think it is deserved.

So, what ushers me into hope these days? It's the love for and from the Creator. It's love for and from my community and love for and from me.

CHAPTER 12

Father's Day

JUNE 2017

It was a bit of a gong show when we "celebrated" Mother's Day last month. Gina, understandably, had a difficult time, so I took the kids, and we tried to give her as much space as she needed. I felt like a rock at the time, but I knew it wasn't "my day"; it was the day to celebrate Gina as a mother. I saw how difficult it was for her, so I wasn't quite sure what to expect for Father's Day.

As the week of Father's Day arrived, I got a message from my mother-in-law, "Hey, the whole family is going up to the cottage this weekend; we'd love it if you and the kiddos would come too." Gina was working afternoons that weekend, so I thought, *what the heck, I might as well be amongst family this weekend. I'm feeling pretty strong, and I think it'll be good to get away and enjoy the kids this weekend.* So, I texted her back, "Sounds good, Mom, we're in."

I messaged Mandy, my sister-in-law, as they were dealing with a colicky baby, "Hey, I'm heading up this weekend, are you? I plan on going up Thursday night, so I can take Aaron with me if you'd like." She readily agreed to me taking their oldest. On Thursday, I dropped by their house, picked up my nephew, and off I went. They were planning on going up Friday night, so I just had to watch him briefly until they came up.

The kids got packed up, and we all loaded into the van for a quiet drive to the cottage. When we got there, we enjoyed supper, and drinks, and I put the kids down to bed. Later that night, Will, Megan, and their kids showed up with their dogs. My in-laws had also gotten a new puppy; a farm dog that was still too young to be left alone on the farm. So, four dogs and five kids were at the cottage that night. I was most worried about the kids, but boy, was I wrong. Three of the dogs, with every other step, pissed and shit all over the floor.

Stresses were already running high when Mandy and Alex showed up with little colicky Eli, and their arrival only intensified the stress. My mother-in-law watched the colicky baby for the rest of the weekend, which normally would be alright, except she usually did everything when people were around. She was the one who would cook, clean up, and make sure everything was running smoothly. With her out of commission, and no one else seemingly lifting a finger, it felt like I did most of the cooking and cleaning up after meals that weekend.

Sunday morning, Father's Day, I walked up the stairs first thing in the morning and started to get breakfast on the table for everyone. I made sure to wish Alex, Will, and my father-in-law a happy Father's Day, to which they all replied, "Thanks." They were all busy with the kids and dogs, too busy to take notice that everything else was being taken care of for them. I cleaned up the breakfast dishes and started packing our stuff so we could leave. Everyone else was leaving later in the day, and they were busy preparing for whatever they had going on that day.

Feeling overwhelmed and a little stressed, I disappeared downstairs into the room that the kids and I were sharing. As I started gathering all our stuff together, my phone rang. It was my mom and sister Denise calling on Face-Time. "Hey, Jay, happy Father's Day!! How are you doing today? We know that this is the first Father's Day without your little guy." I almost completely broke down on the phone right then and there. It was the first time anyone had said that to me that day.

"Thanks," I responded, "I'm just trying to get packed up so we can take off." I got off the phone as quickly as I could, the emotions starting to pick up in me; I gathered the rest of our stuff and brought it to the van. As I stepped outside, the skies opened up, and rain began to fall. I moved the van around so that it was close to the cottage and loaded our stuff in until I could no longer. I sat on the steps, where I slowly began to break down.

I thought of all the things I would never be able to teach Ezra. All the things he would never experience. It just came over me, seemingly out of the blue. I sat there on the front porch watching the sky's tears join mine. I was exhausted, sleep-deprived, and feeling the busyness of serving others the days and nights that came before. As the raindrops joined the drops coming from my eyes, I felt utterly alone and completely worthless.

The house behind me was teeming with life. But for the next 45 minutes, I was sitting on the front steps alone. Nobody even noticed I was gone. I felt unqualified to be a parent, a husband, or a friend. I didn't feel like I could offer anything to anyone. I barely felt that I could offer myself anything. And so, I sat there. Completely surrounded, yet utterly alone.

This wasn't necessarily a new thing for me. I've been surrounded by people I love and who love me – friends, family, and acquaintances – yet, I've felt completely alone. Entirely unqualified to be "playing" the role that I was playing. Completely worthless.

Actually, I live most of my life being on the outside while playing on the inside. My work as a consultant brings me into contact with countless individuals and groups, all of which I belong to for a short period of time, but really, I don't fit in. I'm not from that community; I just get to play someone who is for a short period of time. I did it throughout high school and college as well. I had a core group of friends with whom I could be exactly who I was, but I "belonged" to multiple different groups. The jocks, the partiers, and the nerds all expected me to be one of them, but really, I was just an outsider looking in.

I sat there feeling all those feelings of self-doubt, fear, and unworthiness that I think we all feel sometimes. Sometimes it feels that we are playing the role of father or mother when really, we feel like we can barely take care of ourselves. We say things to ourselves like, "Way to go, Jason...you blew that one. Why do you keep screwing this up? Why can't you get anything right?" Well, if I'm being honest, I usually add a few more swear words into that dialogue.

Sometimes I wonder what it would look like if we talked to others the way we talk to ourselves. If we did that, I think we really would be quite alone.

After sitting on the porch for 45 minutes, I went inside to collect my kids and get on the road. I was soaked from head to toe, but I needed to leave there immediately. My emotions were high, and I was feeling wholly unappreciated and unwelcome. So, it was time to go. I walked into the cottage and asked where Carson and Zoey were. My mother-in-law looked at me, and she must have seen something in my eyes. Maybe it was the puffiness; maybe it was because I was completely wet, who knows. She looked at me and said, "You know, Jason, you're a pretty wonderful father, and all these kids here love you very much."

I said thank you, collected the kids, and took off down the road as quickly as I could. The whole way home, I played back the weekend, getting increasingly upset, but my mother-in-law's words stayed with me. Was I a complete screw-up? Was I just playing the role of a father? Was I worthless?

The next day, I sat in my office mulling all these things over in my mind, and I decided to rid myself of the doubting, fear-mongering voice that lingered in my head. Yes, I decided that it was lying to me. Do I screw up? Sure, do. Do I stick my foot in my mouth? Constantly. Do I take care of myself properly? Not nearly enough as I should. Does that mean I'm not worthy? Not a chance.

As I sat there, I pulled out my notebook and started writing.

I am worthy of spending time on.
I am worthy of being loved.
I am worthy of expressing love.

I am worthy of being listened to.

I am worthy of being a parent.

I am worthy of being a spouse.

I am worthy of being a partner.

I am worthy of being a friend.

I am worthy of serving and being served.

I am worthy of contributing to the greater good.

I am worthy of taking time out of my day to relax and to work.

I am worthy of being a writer and compiling sentences.

I am worthy of serving others even though I am not perfect.

I am worthy of serving a God who doesn't need anything from me.

I am worthy of being saved.

I am worthy of being sad and filled with emotions.

I am worthy of feeling joy and being filled with emotions.

I am worthy of being a conflict management specialist.

I am worthy of walking into my own pain.

I am worthy of singing at the top of my lungs with the windows down.

I am worthy of sitting with others in their time of need and joy.

I am worthy of being a man.

I am worthy.

I am worthy.

I am worthy.

CHAPTER 13

How Are You Really Doing?

JULY 2017

This guy enters a village where a pair of sisters, Mary and Martha, live so they invite him and his entourage to their house. The group gets chatting, and Martha disappears into the kitchen to prepare something to eat and drink. A while later, Martha's still in the kitchen, and it's hard to tell if the smoke coming through the doors is from the food she's cooking or her nasty thoughts.

Martha walks past the kitchen door and glances at her sister Mary, who is just sitting there with the group hanging on every word. You can hear Martha's thoughts – *Pffft...that Mary...does she think this food just prepares itself? Look at her! Just sitting there while I must do all the work preparing for this whole group. And what does she do? Nothing!*

After a while, Martha pops her head into the living room and says to this guy, Jesus, "Uhm...Jesus? don't you care at all that Mary has abandoned me in the kitchen? Tell her to lend me a hand here!"

Jesus looks at her and responds, "Martha, dear Martha, you're fussing far too much and getting yourself worked up over nothing. Only one thing is essential, and Mary has chosen it. It's the main course, and it won't be taken from her" (based on Luke 10: 38-42).

For most of my life, I've been a Martha. I've been the person in the kitchen preparing food, preparing a bed for my guests, and making sure everything is just perfect; by the time it's all ready, I'm far too tired to actually enjoy the presence of my guests.

How often do we do this? We make ourselves so busy that we don't enjoy the people right in front of us. We pack our days full with work, hockey, dance, parties, play-dates, soccer, music lessons, school, and much more. By the end of the day, we're exhausted, and we haven't even stopped to think about anything meaningful.

How often do you ask someone, "Hey! How's it going?" only to hear the response, "I'm good man...really busy these days!" We wear busyness as a badge of honour today in our society. Being busy has become a status symbol, a symbol of great importance.

I know I feel more successful and important when I say I'm busy. That means I'm in demand; that means that people want me, and if people want me, that must mean I'm important.

I think, as men, especially, this busyness is another way for us to hide. It's another mask that we put on so that we don't have to face what's happening inside of us.

I've been thinking about suicide recently and what happens to people who choose to kill themselves. Maybe it's the recent deaths of Chris Cornell and Chester Bennington and how such iconic men, men whom I've looked up to, dealt with their depression. Maybe it's because, in my work life, I've been doing some work in a male-dominated workplace where I can see the many masks people wear: the repression, the (un)health. Maybe it's because I've been ignoring my own emotions and feelings while I wait with great anticipation for a new baby while still grieving the departure of our last.

So when my friend Benji gave me a message this week that said, "Hey... beers this week?" I quickly accepted the invitation and set up a time to meet. That night we walked into the bar, grabbed a seat, and looked over the menus.

"So, how are you doing?" Benji asked me. I replied, "Good...staying pretty busy, you know..."

"No... how are you really doing?"

The question caught me off guard, and I almost broke into tears right then and there.

I don't know what it is about men and emotions; I know a lot of men who would say that their fathers weren't there for them in the way they needed them to be when they were growing up. Unfortunately, this story isn't uncommon and seems rampant throughout our culture. While our dads were there physically, they were emotionally distant. While they ensured that there was food on the table (in most cases), they didn't have the capacity to sit with us when we had a broken heart or a stubbed toe. "Walk it off," they would say, "boys don't cry." "Man up and pull up your panties" were all phrases they would say. In other words, take those emotions and feelings that you're experiencing and stuff them down. Way down, and never bring it up again.

I don't know if it's because of our culture or something else, but men seem to have adopted the mantra that real men aren't weak. Men are strong. They are tough. They take it on the chin and carry on with life. They do not show emotion or tears. They take it like a man. Meaning they stuff it down and don't think about it again.

In my conflict work, I've told many clients, "You can sweep conflict under the rug, but sooner or later, you're going to have a mountain in your living room." The same is with emotions for men (or anyone really). We can sweep those emotions under the rug time and time again, thinking to ourselves that it's not that big a deal.

That comment really stung. Sweep it under the rug. *Why don't my friends call me anymore?* Sweep it under the rug. *I'm worried about my children.* Sweep it under the rug. *I'm stressed beyond belief at work.* Sweep it under the rug. *I feel fat and ugly.* Sweep it under the rug. *My parents are losing their mental capacities.* Sweep it under the rug. *My wife just left.* Sweep it under the rug. *Finances are really tight right now, and I'm going to lose my house.* Sweep it under the rug. *My dog just ran away.* Sweep it under the rug. *My son just died.* Sweep it under the rug.

Only sweeping it under the rug doesn't do anything except compound our problems. We sweep all these things under the rug and then pretend we're doing well like we're still in control, like we're still strong. We wake up and put on our many masks. But pretending to be strong when sitting on a mountainous rug of problems isn't sustainable.

It's the same as being busy, really. We use it as an excuse, another mask that we can walk around in. I'm not saying it's bad to be busy; I'm not saying it's bad to hustle. However, if we don't pause, we also don't take time to reflect. Then we don't take time to care for ourselves. And if we don't take time for ourselves, we can't properly care for others either.

"Everything's good" I keep telling myself. "You're fine, you're good, just keep going."

I hate it when my mind tells me something and my body tells me something different. Our bodies are smart. I know for me; it tells me signs of how I'm really doing. Typically, the feeling starts in my stomach, but occasionally, and especially lately, it tells me in my back and neck when I'm under too much stress.

Just before leaving on vacation, I started feeling pain under my left arm. It started like a chaff; you know when you change deodorants, and your armpit goes all crazy? Yeah, that's what it started as. It hurt, but it was bearable. Then came the shooting pain in my chest. *Oh crap...*I thought...*I have cancer or some sort of heart problem, don't I?* The pain was severe and started to go through my back.

So, I did what I usually do with these kinds of things. I ignored it. *It'll go away...it just needs some time...it just needs some rest.* So, I did just that for a whole week. Then, I went on vacation. Gina and I loaded up the kids and went north to the cottage with my sister, Denise, and her husband, Ryan. The plan was to sit on the dock, watch the kids play in the water, go on a walk or two, drink a few beers, do some fishing, and just relax. I was looking forward to the time away; it had already been a busy summer — way busier than it usually has been in summers past, so we needed the break.

We went up on Friday afternoon after work, and by Saturday, little sores started showing up on my back. "It's probably just allergies," I said, but Gina said I would have to get it checked out when we got back home. I took some Advil and Benadryl for the week to deal with the immense pain throbbing through my body, which seemed to help. The sores started to scab over, and the pain eventually started to subside.

The week was great; Gina and I went into town on Saturday and bought the kids their first fishing rods—an iron man fishing rod for Carson and an "Elsa and Anna" rod for Zoey. We sat at the end of the dock casting into the water, slowly reeling back in, and playing with the worms on the dock.

The kids loved it until they caught a fish. Carson felt a tug on his rod, "Give it a quick tug and then start reeling the rod in nice and evenly," I told him. He was pumped. "Mom! Mom! I caught a fish! I caught a fish!! Oh man!" he screamed at the top of his lungs. When the fish started to come to the surface, his glee turned to fear. "Ahhhh! Daddy! Help! Help!" as he held the rod and fish, swaying back and forth out as far as he possibly could from him. I did everything I could do to stay on the dock; I was laughing so hard.

That week I also got the chance to get out on the kayaks quite a bit, with and without kids. There's something about being on the water that's so peaceful, so relaxing, and so mysterious. When you're on top of the water close to shore, you can see all the fish swimming under you. When you go a little way out from the shore, the water becomes darker, and for a while, I just sat there, wondering what all existed below the surface.

I was out on the water one day and saw the lake's loon. I followed her for a while and watched as she glided graciously through the water, looking so calm on the surface and knowing that her little feet were cutting through the water as fast as a propeller.

I sat there reflecting on something I had heard from James Finley. I'm paraphrasing, but he says, "It's important for us to learn how to float in the shallow water before we venture out to the deep water. That way, we can touch the ground if we get too freaked out. Once we learn to float in the shallow water, we can slowly wade out to deeper waters, knowing we can always return."

I thought back on the past year, knowing that I had indeed learned how to float in the shallow water and that I was in the process of venturing out into the depths, the unknown, looking into the darkness of the water that existed below me as I looked to find out what lived down there.

When we returned home, I went to the doctor as Gina had instructed. The doctor took one quick look at the sores on my back and said, "Yep...that's shingles. Been under some stress in your life recently?" She grinned, knowing about Ezra and that we were in the last month of expecting another baby. "Next time," she said, "don't be such an idiot and come see me right away for help instead of going through all that pain."

"Yes, ma'am," I replied and went on my way back home.

If we're going to gain any insights from our life experiences, we need to live into the pause. Take time to notice the beauty that surrounds us. Take time to notice the pain around us. Take time to truly notice what's happening around us...and in us.

It's time to start being more like Mary, noticing something significant is happening right in front of me, sitting down at the foot of Jesus, and simply taking it all in. Be still, live in the pause, embrace the vulnerable parts of ourselves, engage in curiosity, and venture into those depths so that we can act again.

Our ability to be still and lean into the pause is the starting point for our true growth. As parents. As employees and business owners. As human beings. It's embracing our brokenness and beauty, sitting with the pain and love, and taking the time to simply be. Our ability to be still and lean into the pause is the starting point for our true growth.

I wonder how many lives would be saved if we just paused and surrounded ourselves with people like Benji, asking the question, "How are you really doing?"

I wonder if that would have made a difference in Chris Cornell and Chester Bennington's life. I wonder if that would transform the male-dominated workplace I've been working with. I wonder if we asked that question repeatedly to our male friends if that would help them, and us, to address the mountainous rug we're perched on. I wonder if men acknowledged their feelings a little more, we would see that emotions are not a sign of weakness, but of strength. I wonder if living in the pause and asking that little question could start a revolution.

CHAPTER 14

Anxiety August

AUGUST 2017

August has always been a busy month. It's Carson's birthday, my parents' anniversary, now also Ezra's birthday, and it would be our newest child's birthday too.

We had planned a caesarean section for our fourth, knowing we couldn't go through the unknowns of another labour. We were nervous and excited. This month would become known to Gina and me as Anxiety August.

I wanted to shout for joy. I wanted to shout expletives. I wanted to keep myself busy, put my head down and work, be distracted, and be anywhere but in my body. And yet, I knew that if I didn't sit with it, sit with the pain, the anxiety, and the joy, it would only make matters worse. I felt torn inside, wanting to take the time to marvel at the miracle of childbirth but scared, worried, and nervous that this upcoming child also wouldn't make it.

As Ezra's first birthday approached, our anxiety grew. We were planning on going to the cottage again to get away, to be emotional and with our thoughts, but at the last moment, we heard that we wouldn't be the only ones at the cottage that weekend. "I don't know, babe," I said to Gina, "I don't know if I can do people that weekend. I don't know how this is going to hit me, how it's going to hit us. Both of our anxieties are sky-high right now; maybe we should do something at home."

That same day we got a card from Russ and Melissa. On the inside of the card, they'd written, "We love you so much, and we're so proud of you guys for how you are living your lives and living into Ezra's legacy. Attached is some money for you to buy some balloons for all your kids so that you can celebrate Ezra's first birthday."

As I looked over the card and felt the bills between my hands, instantly, I knew what we needed to do that upcoming weekend. "Alright...see how this lands for you," I said to Gina, "Why don't we go out for breakfast with just us and the kids, go to the party store, buy some balloons, one for Carson and Zoey, and then one for Carson and Zoey to release at Ezra's grave for his birthday. Then, and hear me out here...let's have a birthday party with all the friends that were there at the funeral, and we'll have a big BBQ."

Gina sat there thinking, and tears started coming to her eyes. "That sounds perfect."

By wanting to go to the cottage we realized we were trying to escape something inescapable. Ezra's birthday would come, whether we wanted it or not. He would have been one year old. So instead of avoiding it, let's lean into it. Lean into the discomfort and the sadness to see if we can bring a little joy to those dark places. Our community has meant everything to us over the past year, and it seemed fitting to celebrate and surround ourselves with them.

I went downstairs and started to pray. I prayed for God to watch over this little one that was coming. I prayed for God to ease the discomfort. I prayed for God to give me the courage to sit with the pain and joy. To sit in the deep end and begin exploring the depths. I prayed for God to let me love without fear of being heartbroken again.

The scary thing about love is that it can hurt. It can tear us up inside. I started loving Ezra well before he was born without a breath. When he was born, the wind was completely knocked out of me. I didn't want to love again. It hurt way too damn much. And now, I find myself in a similar position. A new baby is on the way. A baby that (like all the others) I didn't know the gender of — a baby that I've never met outside the womb. A baby that is completely helpless and at the mercy of God knows what.

But at that moment, in that prayer, I decided to choose love. Because that's what true warriors do, they know there are risks, and they love despite those risks. But it's hard. It's really hard. It's hard not knowing. It's hard entering the waves of uncertainty. It's hard putting your head out there again and hoping that it doesn't get chopped off.

So, I'm choosing to trust. Do I know the purpose of why God let this suffering enter my life? Not even close. But does it truly matter? I sense God has used this painful, awful experience in incredible and life-giving ways. He used Ezra to create a legacy I get the privilege and honour to help facilitate. He used Ezra to change me.

So, I'm choosing to trust. Trust in a God who loves me, my family, our new in-the-womb baby, our two kids currently occupying our house and our Ezra. And yes, that trust wavers from time to time. Other times it's like a rock. And at the same time, I've experienced this not knowing. I've experienced that lack of control. So, every day, I wake up and make a choice. A choice to love. A choice to trust. A choice to live in the uncertainty that fogs my mind instead of fighting for control.

A few days later, I sat at home alone the day before Ezra's first birthday. I pulled out my computer and began typing into The Shit Club blog.

Dear Ezra,

Tomorrow will be one year since you were delivered into God's hands, our little devastating blessing. Twelve months have passed without the ability to hold, hug, kiss, and see you grow. Three hundred sixty-five days have painfully started and ended without the ability to see you grow, develop, and show your personality.

I had big plans for you. Plans to teach you about sports, life, and relationships. Plans for you to grow old with your mom, brother, sister, and me. Plans for family vacations and to show you the world and all its beauty. Plans to teach you to go to the bathroom by yourself, ride a bike, and cook a meal. Plans to love you as only a father could.

I couldn't wait to see how you would interact with your siblings, get into trouble, and bring smiles to our faces. I was so excited to laugh at your jokes, see life through your eyes, and see what legacy you would leave.

But there were other plans. Life got in the way. Things happened outside of our control. Things that I'm not a huge fan of, but I'm learning to accept it with the help of God because you are having an impact. You are leaving your legacy on this world. You have forever impacted me, changed me, transformed me. And I hate it. And I love it. I hate that you're not here with me. I hate that I can't just pick you up and give you hugs and kisses. I hate that I can't tickle you and watch you scream hysterically on the floor. I hate that I can't tuck you in each night and read you a story.

And I love that you still speak to me every day. I love that you still visit me in different forms. I love that you flow through my fingers as I write in my journal and on this blog. I love that I can feel your embrace through the warm wind across my neck, the stars in the sky, and the words others speak. I love that you are still as present as the day you were born into the hands of God.

But you must know that we all, your mother, brother, sister, and me, miss you with all our hearts. We talk about you all the time. We cry about you all the time. Our hearts break as we sing songs about you and look at the empty chair around our dinner table. As we let our imaginations float to what you would have been like and what you're doing now that you're chilling out with God.

I can't explain how much it hurts not to have you here. The words can't find their way out. I can't explain the impact you have already had on me. As a father, as a husband, as a brother, as a human being... you've changed me as only a son could. You've taught me lessons so engrained in me that they bleed from my heart and shoot through my veins. Lessons that I have only begun to mine the depths of. Lessons that shake me to my very core.

You taught us all about love. The beauty of love. The heartbreak of love. The risks of love. You taught us that we couldn't control everything and that we must step out of our comfort zone and trust. Trust those around us. Trust in God. Trust that whatever comes our way, no matter how wonderful or complex, there is a God who loves us unconditionally.

I can't thank you enough for teaching me what you have taught me. I can't thank you enough for making me a better person. I can't thank you enough for being with us for the short time you were.

And I miss you so much. Tomorrow we're going to visit where we lay you. And we will release some balloons for you, hoping they find you on your earthly birthday. And we'll shed some tears because you won't join us physically. And then we're going to surround ourselves with people that love us and that we love so much. And we're going to have a toast in your honor. And I'm going to be a fucking mess through the whole thing...even if I don't show it the whole time. But that's okay because I miss you more than anything I've ever experienced.

And I'll be here all day, patiently waiting to feel your presence. Feel your message of love that you'll show through the wind and birds, God's *creation, and those around us. I'll be here thinking about you, dreaming about you, and loving you.*

You truly have been our devastating blessing, and I'm so proud to call you my son.

With all the love of my being,
Dad

My finger hovered over the publish button. Do I dare share this with my community? Do I dare be this raw? This exposed? This vulnerable? I felt a gentle nudge, almost like Ezra told me, "Just post it, Dad; I want to read it."

So, I hit publish, closed the computer, and wiped my eyes. I put on my shoes and went for a walk. A walk so I could see the sun, hear the birds, and feel the wind gently caress my cheek.

I didn't sleep much that night, so I was up early. I ran to the gym before anyone else got up to get some energy and nerves out. We got our stuff together when I got back, packed the van, and went out for breakfast. There weren't a lot of words spoken that morning; everyone was on the verge of tears.

We ordered our food and talked with the kids about the party store we would go to after breakfast and all the other plans for that day. It was a special day, but honestly, I wasn't sure if I should call it a birthday or an anniversary. It was both of those things.

Today was the day Ezra would have turned one, and instead of celebrating him with us, we celebrate the impact he has had on us. So, we sat at breakfast, ordering food for four instead of five people. The waitress, trying to make small talk as we paid our bill, asked us innocently, "So what's on the agenda for today, folks?"

Before Gina or I could respond, Carson piped up, "Well, it's going to be a busy day! We're going to get some balloons for my brother and release them at his grave. He's dead, and it's his birthday today! Then we'll have friends over today and have a big BBQ!"

The waitress took it all in and tried to preserve her calm and cool appearance, but you could tell she was uncomfortable, wanting to get out of the landmine she had just stepped on. Gina and I just smiled at her, thanked her for bringing us our meal and went to the party store.

No matter the occasion, bringing kids to a party store is pretty difficult. There are just too many amazing things that seemingly explode the kids' minds. Things, of course, that they need to have right at that moment. We managed to direct their attention long enough for each of them to pick out a balloon they wanted to bring home and a balloon they could release at the grave. Carson picked an iron man balloon for himself and a balloon for Ezra with a blue outer circle depicting cars and trucks on it. The middle had a train that carried the number 1 that said "birthday boy" on it. Zoey had to have Rainbow Dash from My Little Ponies, and for Ezra, she picked a white balloon with a beautiful rainbow and sun stretched across it with a joyous "Happy 1st birthday!" written underneath the rainbow.

We piled back into the van, put the balloons in the back, and went to the cemetery. It was hard to get out of the van, but somehow, we managed to put one foot in front of the other and make our way to Ezra's grave. We crept down and picked away some grass that crept onto Ezra's nameplate. The kids ran around with the balloons playing balloon tag, and I sat there wondering if our kids would grow up to view cemeteries differently than how I did.

Cemeteries have always fascinated me as they present all the history and legacies each individual has left before us. I wonder if my kids will remember the times they played while we were there at the cemetery. I wonder if my kids will remember the tears they shed there, the hugs, the kisses. I wonder if they'll remember the day all our friends and family were there as we laid Ezra into the ground. I wonder if they'll remember the many times we've laughed while sitting beside Ezra's grave.

We tied the two balloons together, and all of us held on. I wish I could have taken a picture. Two big hands and two little hands anxiously grasping at the strands of string, not wanting to let go, wishing that these balloons were coming home with us. Wishing we were sitting at home opening presents. And yet, here we were, grasping onto the strands of strings in the middle of the cemetery. "1, 2, 3, let go!" We all counted together, and the balloons soared into the sky. We sat back in the grass. We cried. We caressed each other's cheeks and backs as we lay back to watch the balloons go further and further into the sky towards the clouds. "Do you think they'll find Ezra?" Carson asked.

"You bet they will," I said.

We watched the balloons until they were a speck in the grandiose sky. We watched as they floated into the clouds until they were finally gone. I feel like we put all our thoughts, birthday wishes, and love into those balloons and set them free so that when they reached the other side, Ezra could look through them and receive all the hugs and kisses we so deeply wanted to give him.

We went home and got ready for the afternoon's festivities, cutting the grass, sweeping the deck and porch, and cleaning up the dog poop lying around. Then the people came. All at once. It was as if they had planned it down to the second. Our house went from being quiet and sombre to vibrant and full of life. Kids ran in every direction while the guys sat on the deck drinking beer, and the women disappeared into the house.

Parts of it reminded me of these same people gathering one year ago at the farm after Ezra's funeral, and here they were again, bringing joy and celebration, all while being willing to sit in the grief and devastation.

As we sat around, ate together, drank together, laughed together, cried together, I could only think one thought. This is community. This is what community looks like. This is what it looks like for a community to love. This is what it looks like for a community to grieve. This is what it looks like for a community to celebrate. This is what a true community looks like.

No one said anything special, brought anything special or did anything special. And yet, everything about it was special. It was people's presence, their willingness to enter a space and be impacted by it. It was their willingness to enter a love that simultaneously gave and took. It's a love that isn't conditional on saying or doing the right thing. It's a love that shows up and sits in the joy and the crap. It's the closest thing to true love that I have experienced.

And it's risky love. That's one thing that Ezra has taught me this past year. Love is risky. We invest all these feelings into another person, and there is always a risk that we will walk away with our hearts broken. Love is risky because we risk being changed by our experiences and the experiences of others. So, we often enter in not from a place of risky, deep love but shallow love. But not today. Not this community of people. Not this family.

Today everyone showed up, willing to take the risk of love, knowing full well that true love is being willing to be changed by our experiences and the experience of others. And it's worth it.

The time had come for the scheduled caesarean section where our fourth child was to be born. I packed up and piled the kids and their stuff into the car and brought them to my in-laws. We told our family and some friends about the date but couldn't bring ourselves to tell our children. They were anxious enough already; we didn't need them to carry this weight as well. I kissed and hugged them while praying that I would be calling them with good news. On the way home, I decided it would be a good idea to put on the 'pump-up jams' to get into the right mindset. It felt like I had to get myself hyped up for the day. After all, I knew I would need all the strength and energy I could muster because my mind was full of questions.

It was a weird experience, knowing in advance the day that your child would be born. Knowing about your new child's birthday before they were born into this world. You could feel the anxiety and tension that led up to that day. I was excited for another child, yet my stomach twisted and turned in ways I had never experienced before. All kinds of thoughts ran through my mind: *What if this baby doesn't make it either? What if something happens to my wife? What if there are complications? What if....? What if....?*

The song changed to Volbeat's "A Warrior's Call," one of my go-to pump-up songs. I turned it up to an ear-bleeding level. I could feel the guitar and bass in my chest. I mouthed the words as they were chanted: "Feel the power of a warrior! Fight, fight, fight, fight. Let's get ready to rumble! Fight, fight, fight, fight." I could feel tears coming, so I started praying. *Hey God...so...today's the big day. I don't know how today is going to go. Last time didn't end so well... either way God, I trust you. I know you'll be there regardless of the outcome.*

An overwhelming sense of calm came over me. A calm like I had never experienced before. A full surrender of control, letting go of all that anxiety, stress, and plans I had for our lives. I gave it all over—fully emptying everything I was holding onto.

That morning, August 28th, we rolled into the hospital at 9:00 a.m. and sat in the delivery room. A nurse came in with hospital gowns for my wife and scrubs for me. "Can we check the baby?" my wife asked, "I need to hear the heartbeat. The nurse looked at us, and her eyes said it all. "Lady, in two hours you will not only hear the heartbeat, but you'll be also holding your freaking baby! Your request is ridiculous! You know how many things I must do before we get ready for this c-section?"

She didn't say much and left the room. A few minutes later, she came back. "I'm so sorry," she said, "I just read your file and saw that you lost a child last year. Of course, we can put on the monitors for you to hear the baby if that's what you want. I didn't realize..."

So, we sat there listening to baby's heartbeat. *Whoosh, whoosh, whoosh,* the song that never sang just a year prior.

The midwives came, hugged us, and brought Gina down to the O.R. Oddly; the hospital was running ahead of schedule that day, so we were in the surgical room early. I waited outside while they prepared the room and my wife for surgery.

As I sat in the waiting room, I noticed that calm come over me again. I wasn't anxious. I wasn't trying to control anything. I knew I had prepared myself and my family to the best of my abilities, and now I had to trust. I had let go of anything I was holding onto and put my full trust that, regardless of the outcome, we would be held in love.

After what seemed like hours, I was called into Gina's room. I sat behind the curtain that separated her head from the rest of her body, and I looked into my wife's eyes. So much joy, fear, excitement, and overwhelming peace filled those eyes. We sat there for a few minutes while people whirled around the room, and before I knew it, I was told that I could announce the gender of the baby.

As I stood up to peer over the curtain, I heard her—the sound I had longed for, the cry of a baby. And then I saw her being held in the hands of the doctor. It was our baby. Our "rainbow" child. Our fourth beautiful child. A little girl.

The doctors and midwives looked her over, wrote out her stats, and placed her on Gina's chest. Born at 11:11. A wish come true.

There she lay, her little body full of life, snuggled into my wife's chest. They both lay there with their eyes closed, savouring the moment they could connect on this side of the womb. Their breath was no longer rapid but settling into a deep meditative pattern as they relished the physical connection. And there I stood, watching my two girls fall deeper in love. Tears began to roll down my cheeks. I no longer saw all the people hustling around the room; I no longer heard the beeps of the machines; it all fell into the background. There was our daughter. A gift from God. Our little Norah Rie.

It was a moment of pure joy and fear. Love and loss. Hope and despair. It was the first time that I realized how they started to connect. When we journey into the depths, the muck, the shit, it is there that we learn the most about love. It is there that we learn the most about joy and hope. AND we don't fully know fear, loss, and despair without knowing and experiencing unbridled love. To suffer is to love, and to love is to suffer.

A little over a year ago, those phone calls to our friends and family were so painful, and this time so full of joy. People came to pour out their love the same way they did the year prior, just taking a slightly different form this time.

Our journey was far from over. The anxiety, the grief, and the devastation hadn't left us. People always tell us, "Time heals all," but, really, it doesn't heal anything. Time didn't help us or make it easier, but we got a little better at sitting with it somewhere along the line.

That night, after everyone was gone, we tucked her in and sang together,

Now I lay me down to sleep
I pray the Lord my soul to keep
Guide me through the starry night
And wake me when the sun shines bright.

Now I lay me down to sleep
I pray the Lord my soul to keep
If I die before I wake
I pray the Lord my soul to take.

Amen.

Epilogue

Seven years after losing one of my children, I still don't know whether or not to call August 12th his birthday or his death anniversary. Maybe we should create a new word that would highlight both the celebration of a birth and the mourning that still exists for the passing of a child. Birthsary? Anniversaday? Either way, I'll be honest, I still feel a little stupid whenever the 12th of August comes around, and I'm trying to explain the mixed emotions that comes with celebrating birth and mourning death. In many ways, I think it sums up grief. We think we're supposed to know how it goes, how we're supposed to feel, how we're supposed to deal with these complex emotions that love has left us with, but it's a clusterfuck. There is no right answer when it comes to grief. There is no right feeling. There is joy and celebration: darkness and anguish. And if you're fortunate, all those feelings come at once.

Over the last couple of years, the opportunity to talk about my son, Ezra, in keynotes across the country has emerged—specifically relating to the next stage of dealing with/processing a pandemic. I've been able to talk about what I've learned about emotional resilience and how we can start to process grief. Sitting up on a stage in front of hundreds of people and telling stories about your living and dead children has been interesting and admittedly weird, and I've loved every minute of it.

Let me explain that last sentence a little further: I have loved the opportunity to talk about ALL of my children. To talk about what my children have taught me, how they've shaped me, and how I've tried to shape them. I've loved sharing the memory of Ezra, the impact that Ezra has made on me and the people around me, and how we continue to preserve his legacy. I have loved the people I have met on this journey and the knowledge that I'm not alone in this terrible club.

So, I have loved aspects of sharing my story, and yet, I wish I never had this story to tell in the first place. People often say, "It must be amazing to turn this tragedy into something beautiful—you're so strong; I could never be that strong." I struggle with these comments for two reasons: The first is that I wouldn't wish this experience on my worst enemy, so no... I wouldn't voluntarily go down this road again if given the option. Am I glad that I've found purpose and, dare I say, meaning out of this hell-filled experience? Absolutely. Getting to go up on stages around the country and talk about my children is amazing. The ability to journey alongside individuals and couples in their grief, walking side-by-side to unpack, explore, and navigate those murky and complex experiences, is some of the most life-giving work I have ever done. Would I trade it all to be able to touch, hold, see, and, yes, even smell my son? Absolutely.

The second is that I'm not stronger than anyone else. You would be, and are, just as strong. You don't have another choice. The choices at that point are slim; if you desire to live, you don't have a choice but to put one foot in front of the other. It's not strength; it's survival. There have been many moments over the years where I've thought about death. Not in the, I'm going to go do this, kind of way, but rather the "if it happened at this moment," I wouldn't be upset. It's not strength; it's survival.

They say that as long as you love, you'll grieve. I completely subscribe to that. Seven years later, I'm still grieving; it just looks different. When you first lose your loved one, grief takes up your entire life. I think people used to think that grief gets easier to deal with over time because it begins to shrink the longer it exists, but that's not the case. Time doesn't heal grief. We need to feel to heal. The only way to the other side of grief is to go through it. So over time, our grief doesn't get smaller; instead, our life grows around it as we learn how to process and experience it.

Seven years later, one of the things that I've learned is that there is less either/or in the world than I had ever thought. We are told that we can do this OR do that. We can either have this or that, but not both. I remember as a kid, we would go to my Opa and Oma's house for birthday celebrations and we'd have cake. It was never enough to have one cake, so often we had a couple! When I'd ask my Opa what kind of cake he would like with his coffee, he'd always say, "A little of both, please," with a mischievous smile on his face. He knew we often position these questions with a bit of either/or, and he would have none of it. I've realized over the years of grief, both from my own experience and through the experience of others, that my Opa was right. The either/or that is presented is typically never the only option available to you. Rather, it's a both/and—a lesson that I've learned time and time again in both my professional and personal life. Life is beautiful and brutal. We get it all; the good and the bad. There is no either/or. We get to experience those beautiful moments that bring a tear to our eye, make our chest pump out with pride, or cause us to think we had an ab workout because we've been laughing so hard. Just recently, I witnessed the graduation of one of my nieces and, that evening I experienced all those feelings. AND life is full of brutal moments. Those moments that take our breath away, leave us feeling empty and in excruciating pain, or our heart being ripped out of our chest. Then there is everything in between. And sometimes, we experience those moments at precisely the same time.

I'll give you a small example. When writing this, my family and I are moving from our little village to a new life adventure three and a half hours north. We've always wanted to do it, so we are excited beyond belief. It allows us to have lakes at our fingertips, spend more time outside, and have a more reasonable pace of life. And yet, we leave behind a neighbourhood that we love, friends and family that we'd do anything for, and a life that we have loved. It's both exciting and sad. Bitter and sweet. Often those experiences and feelings come to me at the same time. This past weekend, as I talked to one of my best friends, I excitedly told him about the latest developments of the move, all while feeling the tears well up in my eyes at the thought of leaving.

Seven years later, grief still comes in waves. When we first lost our son, grief was like a tsunami that came out of nowhere and almost swept me along with it. These days, it's mostly like sitting by a lake. Every now and then, a boat goes past, creating some waves that ripple to the shore. The bigger the boat that goes past, the bigger the wave it creates. So, when I'm out in the water, I bring a few floaties with me in case the waves get too overwhelming or intimidating. Then I can choose whether I need to ride the wave, crash through it, or let it calmly bob me up and down in the water. Other days, it catches me by surprise, and as the wave crashes down on my head and I come up spitting and coughing out water, I desperately search for the floaties I've brought out. As I navigate the waters of grief, it continues to teach me about myself and encourages me to develop patience and gentle compassion for both myself and others.

Shortly after losing our son, I remember going down a Google black hole looking for resources that might help me. Not much existed then, and the existing ones were primarily for women and moms. There are certainly more resources now, yet, they are still primarily focused on female-identifying folks. While I am glad considerably more resources exist for this population, I am also sad and frustrated that there are not more resources for men and male-identifying folks. I've had the pleasure and honour of being one of North America's first male-identifying Pregnancy and Infant Loss Grief Coaches. I've had the incredible honour of holding space for folks from all walks of life and journeying alongside them through their loss and grief. As I've worked with birthing and non-birthing folks impacted by pregnancy and infant loss, I've started to see more and more walls break down. I've started to see more and more individuals step into the unknown and the difficulties of journeying with their emotions and figuring out how to float in the sea of uncomfortableness. And yet, while it is an honour continuing to serve this community, more men need to step into this space. Not to lead, not to change services and supports that already exist, but to be a support for one another. To be a safe place for folks to be honest in their emotions, embracing the complexity of grief and love. This will make us stronger in who we are, strengthen our ties to the community and each other, and better assist us in supporting and serving our birthing partners.

Life is brutal; life is beautiful. We're in this together.

About the Author

Jason Dykstra is a father to four (three living) and helper to many. As an international speaker, trainer, and coach he specializes in the areas of grief, conflict, and communication. He is a Certified Pregnancy and Infant Loss Grief Coach, Certified Mediator, and holds a Masters in Leadership. He lives with his family in the Muskokas in Ontario, Canada. You can visit him online at www.jasondyk.com.

Manufactured by Amazon.ca
Bolton, ON

38474450R00096